Names printed with an asterisk (*) have been changed.

Copyright © 2022 by Latonya Howell

All rights reserved. No part of this book may be reproduced in any manner whatsoever without written permission except in the case of brief quotations embodied in critical articles and reviews.

First Printing, 2022

THE TRAUMA WAS NECESSARY

The Trauma Was Necessary

My Story

LATONYA HOWELL

CONTENTS

| one |

Hello Trauma

What is trauma? Simply put, trauma is our emotional response to a terrible event. It has both immediate and long-term reactions. It impacts our emotions, our relationships, and even manifests itself through physical symptoms. Trauma can paralyze us by preventing us from moving forward in life. For most of us, trauma enters our lives at an early age. It doesn't knock on the door, and it doesn't ask permission to disrupt your entire life; it just simply happens.

I was born into trauma on Thursday, July 31st, 1986, in Pontiac, Illinois at St. James Hospital. My mother was a drug addict and schizophrenic who ran off to Chicago at the age of eighteen to follow who she thought was the love of her life, only to be forced into prostitution. She was incarcerated when I was born and as a result, I went right into foster care. No motherly bonding time, no cute "first outfit," and not a single birth picture. The only thing I have from my birth is a note from my nurse discussing some sort of spots that I was born with on my legs.

I never knew my father, but my mother has always had nothing but good things to say about him; she would always tell me, "He was a good, good man." According to my mother, my father broke up with her after he walked in on her shooting up dope in the bathroom at his house. He asked no questions, and he gave her no opportunities to explain herself. He was just done, their relationship ended in that very moment. One of the only things I know about my father is that he was trained in martial arts and his fists were listed as registered weapons in the state of Illinois. Unfortunately, my father was shot and killed a few years after he discovered my mom shooting up dope, and he never knew I existed. This series of events that happened before I was even alive and when I was too young to know anything, set the foundation and the tone for the beginning of my life. Life was unfair before I even knew I was alive.

My earliest childhood memory was between the ages of three and five. I was living with my mother in an apartment at that time. I had just woken up and she was in the kitchen cooking breakfast. I noticed my backpack was sitting by the door; it was one of those red, blue, and yellow children's backpacks that all children had in the 80's and 90's. My mother was crying as she cooked, and I remember wondering what was wrong with her. She picked me up and began to hug me and explain that I was going away. I remember feeling confused and not understanding what was going on. Then there was a knock on the door. It was a Caucasian lady, with red-rimmed glasses. I came to know this woman as Ms. Sally. She was the first social worker I remember, and I stayed under her care for several years.

My mother handed Ms. Sally the backpack, picked me up and hugged me, and tears poured down her cheeks as she handed me to Ms. Sally. I immediately begin to cry, scream, and kick. My mother just stood there looking helplessly at me. Ms. Sally put me into the back of a white van, and as we drove off, I remember looking behind me and seeing my mother standing in the middle of the street crying. I was reaching and crying for her. I didn't know it at the time, but my mother was returning to prison, and I was re-entering foster care. That memory is ingrained in my mind. Over thirty years later, if I close my eyes, I can envision it as if it happened yesterday.

Trauma impacts us in so many ways. Some of the effects of trauma are immediate. Denial, grief, and other effects of trauma are more long-term, and they impact our thinking patterns and our relationships long after the trauma has occurred. I was well into my twenties before I realized that I was still fighting the effects of what happened to me. Throughout my childhood, I was moved from foster home to foster home as my mom went in and out of prison. Moving around from home to home caused me to have feelings of being unwanted. Was I not good enough for anyone?

At an early age, I began dealing with rejection. I felt rejected by my mom. I didn't understand addiction at the time; I just understood that my mom wasn't there. As I moved around from home to home, I felt more and more unwanted and rejected. I even had a foster mom tell me that nobody wanted me because I would eventually turn out to be just like my mother. By the time that I was five, I had been born in a prison hospital, placed into foster care, allowed to live with my mom again, tragically taken from my mom, and moved in and out of multiple foster homes. Trauma had not only knocked on my door, but it had also bulldozed my entire existence.

Some trauma follows us from one generation to another. We often hear phrases referencing the patterns of sin that show up in families, generation after generation. We hear these patterns referred to as "generational curses," "strongholds", and "familiar spirits." These are thought to be the reasons why things like teenage pregnancy, addiction, and abuse continue from one generation to the next.

Some of the trials we deal with in life result from the actions of our ancestors and have little to do with us. In my bloodline, most of the women, for several generations, were never married, had teenage pregnancies, multiple children by different fathers, drug and alcohol addiction, and prostitution. There was also a strong presence of mental illness. These are things that I was born into and if I wasn't careful, these are things that could be hindrances in my life. Understanding what runs in your family gives you an advantage in handling trauma, because it can give you some insight into what you may face. It can also show you what to avoid so that you don't run into the same issues. I witnessed the struggles that my mom had with drug addiction, so as a result, I had a natural aversion to doing hard drugs. We have the power to fight against the things that have followed our bloodlines for generations. We are called to break generational curses and as a result, we sometimes experience opposition.

"I will bless those who bless you and curse those who treat you with contempt. All the families on earth will be blessed through you." Genesis 12:3 NLT

We constantly hear older generations give younger generations a hard time. They may say, "They are too rebellious, they ask too many questions, they are just so different." As a millennial, I believe that these things are true. Let me respectfully remind you that Jesus Himself was considered "rebellious!" While Jesus walked this earth, there was a group of people called the Pharisees. These people were the perfect definition of "high and mighty." They referred to the Bible often and followed all the many legalistic rules. They should have been exactly who Jesus spent time with, right? Wrong! Jesus wanted nothing to do with those people. They were so caught up in their laws and traditions, that when Jesus performed miracles, they didn't recognize the power of God. Their focus instead, was on the fact that Jesus was performing miracles on the Sabbath. They missed the point big time, and in fact, they were the people who wanted Jesus crucified. Jesus was not quiet, timid, or submissive in His response to the Pharisees.

"Woe to you, teachers of the law and Pharisees, you hypocrites! You give a tenth of your spices-- mint, dill, and cumin. But you have neglected the more important matters of the law-- justice, mercy and faithfulness. You should have practiced the latter, without neglecting the former."

Matthew 23:23 NIV

Jesus rebelled against them, but He did it in a good way, and for a good purpose. You can read all about the Pharisees in the Bible and how they attempted to come for Jesus repeatedly, but they received the ultimate shutdown every time. Jesus was a gangsta in His own way. So, the next time you are referred to as being 'rebellious,' let the people know you learned it from the best, you learned it from Jesus.

I believe that we were given rebellious spirits because we are the chosen generation to break the cycle that has kept our bloodlines in bondage for so long. I'm very much still learning and figuring myself out, but one thing I have learned is that God has equipped my personality with everything that I need. My goal is to be so immersed in the power of God that anything that comes to harm me, or my future generations will have to bow in the presence of God. I declare that teenage pregnancy, drug abuse, prostitution, mental illness - it all stops with me. It no longer has a place in my bloodline. The enemy got the right one this time… he got the rebellious one. You know something, you too can declare and speak over your life and the lives of your future generations.

Being a generational curse breaker is available to all of us. It is simply a decision we make to not fall into the same patterns and habits that our loved ones did. Knowledge is power, and as Maya Angelou once said, "You can't really know where you are going until you know where you have been." What generational curses run in your family? If it's financial, be intentional about research-ing credit and saving. If it's unwed pregnancies, consider becoming abstinent from sex until you are married. We don't have to follow in all the footsteps of our ancestors. Honor their legacies by making choices that are pleasing to God. Why learn the hard way when the outcome of that path has already been revealed to you?!

Some people find it easy to blame every misfortune, sin, and problem on a generational curse. That is not the case at all. I realized at an early age that I couldn't blame generational curses or strongholds on everything that happened in my life. I couldn't play the victim forever.

"Some became fools through their rebellious ways and suffered afflic-tion because of their iniquities." (Psalms 107:17 NIV)

That's being rebellious in a negative way - opposing the truth. It's natural to look for a scapegoat, or someone else to blame when bad things happen to us. Some of us *choose* to live in this mindset permanently.

So, you've been in three relationships in the last three years and all of *them* were the problem? Your mom abandoned you as a child and that's the reason why, in your thirties, you have a bad attitude with everyone and can't control your emotions?

"And *you will* know *the truth,* and *the truth will set you free."* (John 8:32 NLT)

So, I want you to know that some of your trauma is your own doing. There you have it, be free. This was the case for me with certain circumstances. Part of our healing from trauma comes from holding ourselves accountable and sitting in the mess that we created.

Regardless of how our trauma comes about, at some point the responsibility of healing from that trauma becomes our own. You may never get the apology you deserve. Read that again; it's hard, but it's reality. There are certain situations in your life, where you are beyond owed an apology, and you will NEVER get it. What do you do in those situations? I faced several of those issues, one of which was with a close family member. I harbored a lot of pain and hurt towards this person, but I also knew that a conversation was just not possible. I had tried and knew that this person would not carry any accountability for the pain that they caused. I also knew that I could not continue to carry unforgiveness for this person when they had not a care or concern about the issue. So, I wrote them a letter in my journal. The letter started off as more of a venting session, but by the time I wrote the words, "I forgive you anyway," I was overwhelmed with the amount of peace I experienced. I knew immediately that I had experienced a breakthrough in my healing process.

We can only blame other people for our issues but for so long. I came to the realization that what happened to me as a child couldn't be my excuse in my twenties and even now in my thirties. Choosing to forgive, despite not receiving an apology, was one of the first steps towards healing. I might not have been the cause of the trauma, but I was responsible for healing from it.

We've all heard the saying, "Life is what you make it." The statement is partially true. We don't get a choice in so many of the things that happen in life but how we respond to those things can literally make or break us. When you experience trauma, you will often find yourself at a crossroads. That crossroad has to do with your outlook, and yes, it's your choice. So here you are, having dealt with trauma, and you find yourself at a fork in the road. To the right, you have sunshine and to the left, there's rain and thunder. It sounds so cliche, but you can choose to face your trauma with either a positive or negative outlook. I'll discuss this in more detail later but believe me when I say that *choosing* to be positive has saved my life.

| two |

Missing Childhood

After Ms. Sally picked me up from my mother's house, she took me to a foster home with a woman named Mrs. Houston*. I specifically remember driving around the corner from where my mom lived and being dropped off. When I got older and started going to school, I walked past the apartment everyday where I had last lived with my mother. I literally relived the trauma of being taken away from my mother almost every day.

Mrs. Houston was a widowed woman who took in several foster kids. At the time, she had one other foster child who was thought to be developmentally challenged, named Robin*. Early on in my stay, Robin* would do things intentionally to get me in trouble, things like eating foods we weren't supposed to and then blame it on me or break something and then blame it on me. While I would be getting in trouble for her actions, she would look at me and smirk. Robin was several years older than me at sixteen or seventeen. I started to notice that even when I knew that Mrs. Houston knew I wasn't guilty of things, I would still get in trouble. At the time, I wasn't sure why I would still get in trouble for things that Mrs. Houston knew I didn't do.

As a result, I grew to despise living in the same house as Robin. She bullied me physically and verbally, and she knew that she would get away with it. Robin would start by getting me in trouble for small things, but eventually those small things would become major, life-changing events with huge consequences. I stayed with Mrs. Houston for several years in what would be the most difficult years of my childhood, and this was when I experienced the most trauma as a child: trauma inflicted by someone else.

Foster children rotated in and out of Mrs. Houston's house, except for Robin and me, as we seemed to be the only permanent children. One day, a young boy arrived; he was really sad, and he said that his mother would be coming to get him soon. He spent most of his days sitting on the couch and staring out the window. He wouldn't play, he would barely speak, only to say that his mom was coming to get him soon. One day, I sat in the living room and watched him stare out the window for quite some time. By this time, I hadn't seen my own mother for quite some time. I was still very young, five or six years old, but I remember getting so mad at this little boy. He mentioned something to me about his mother coming to get him soon and I snapped at him: "She's not coming. They don't love us, and they don't care!" I remember feeling so confused by my reaction. I knew, as a young child, that I was upset about my own mother not coming to get me, but I also didn't understand how to express what I was feeling. I was wrong though, because a few days later, his social worker came to get him. I never saw him again, but I pray that he was indeed reunited with his mother, and that his life turned out great.

While a lot of our trauma is emotional and leaves scars that aren't visible, some of the trauma we experience is physical and it leaves visual damage and visible scars. One day, I was sitting in the kitchen with Mrs. Houston. It was a cold fall day, as I remember the leaves had turned colors and were covering most of the yard.

I was waiting for hot chocolate to come out of the microwave; I remember feeling so excited for this hot chocolate. Mrs. Houston removed the hot chocolate from the microwave and sat it in front of me. Immediately I bumped the mug and it landed on my lap. I started to scream. Mrs. Houston picked me up and took me into the bathroom, and she sat me on the toilet. I must have passed out from the pain because the next thing I remembered; I was waking up in an ambulance. I had third degree burns on my left leg and second degree burns on my right leg and ended up being in the hospital for quite some time. They made me take baths in this big, round, stainless steel tub. I remember the pain, the bandages, and the long recovery. I still have the scars on both of my thighs to this day. I had to get skin grafts to help the scars heal. Every time I look at them, I am reminded of the trauma and the story behind them. I'm also reminded of a time in my life that I would give anything to forget.

(Trigger Warner (TW)): Sexual Violence

Mrs. Houston had a brother who lived a few houses up the street, and her brother had a son who was in his early teenage years, Mrs. Houston's nephew. The nephew was responsible for walking me to and from the bus stop. At the time, I was maybe six years old. The bus stop was only a couple of blocks away from our houses. We would spend the walk talking. He became someone that I really trusted. I was so young and innocent. The family trusted him with me as well since he eventually became the go-to babysitter for me.

I don't know when between him walking me to and from school, and babysitting me that the sexual abuse started, but I know that I began to fear being him around him. Perhaps during our walking and talking he had made comments that made me uncomfortable. I'm not sure, but I do remember the first time that he raped me. It was fall; I remember because the weather was cool, and the leaves had changed colors. Fall season carried a lot of traumas for me.

I went to school earlier that day and I was playing with another foster kid in the backyard on the swing set. I remember being very uncomfortable; his mood was different, almost aggressive. He was saying things to me that I didn't fully understand but those things made me feel uncomfortable. I just remember wanting to get away from him. I went into the house to use the restroom, he followed me and waited outside the door. I locked the door and stayed in the restroom for as long as possible, hoping that he would go away. Finally, I left the restroom and attempted to sneak into my room to hide, which was to the left of the restroom. There were bunk beds in the room, and the covers on the bed were blue. I locked the door behind me. Even still, he was able to enter the room, and that's when it happened. I just laid there staring at part of the blue cover that was hanging over the edge of the bunk bed, then at the ceiling, then at the bunk bed. I felt so dark and empty inside, not fully understanding what had happened to me, but at the same time feeling gross.

(TW-End)

I was different after that; I saw the world differently. I was about six at the time, and my innocence had been stripped from me. I was no longer the inquisitive, talkative little girl that I had once been. I was quiet and withdrawn. This trauma rocked me to my core. Yet, I didn't tell anyone for a long time. I had now been at Mrs. Houston's house for years now, and I had stability, the most I had ever experienced. I feared that telling someone would remove that stability from my life. I desired to be in a family, and at that time any family would have been acceptable.

By this time, my mother had landed herself in federal prison. I would go and visit her every other week. My mother spent years of my childhood in and out of prison. The prison she was in at this time was a long drive, and the trip literally took most of the day. Ms. Sally and I would leave Mrs. Houston's house early in the morning and drive for hours, visit with my mom for a few hours and then drive home. At the time, I didn't realize that my mom was in prison. I just knew that I couldn't stay with her, and she couldn't leave with me. The adults in my life did a great job of shielding me from what was really going on. Most of my visits were outside on a playground. I remember sitting and eating lunch at a metal bench. I always took lunch with me on visiting days, and it always had to be my favorite sandwich. It was Miracle Whip, American Cheese, and mustard on white bread. No meat, just bread and condiments, and I was serious about that sandwich. I distinctly remember throwing a fit one day over not having that particular sandwich.

The first time I started realizing that my visits with my mom were not normal was the first time we had a visit inside the prison. I remember the smell of bleach, the gray cement walls, and the white tile floors with gray triangles. I still didn't realize it was a prison, and I'm not sure that I even knew what a prison was at the time. I just knew that it was different and that it wasn't normal for a child to visit their parents like this. I loved my mom, and I was always so happy to see her.

Around the age of seven, my mother was released from prison. She moved into her own place. It was a little white house on a quiet road a few doors down from a gas station. I was allowed to visit her there. Our visits consisted of watching television and eating my mom's favorite snack of Lays Potato chips and sour cream dip. Occasionally, I still crave that snack, and I'm instantly reminded of my home visits with my mom. I loved being with my mom; there was no better feeling than being with her. I felt safe with my mom; it was my escape from the continued sexual abuse. My mom would tell me how hard she was trying to get better from her addiction, she told me that she couldn't give me up and that she would continue to fight for me. Her words brought so much comfort to me, but somehow, deep down inside, I knew that we would never live under the same roof again. The visits continued for a while and then they changed to overnight stays once a week. My mother continually promised me that I would be coming home to live with her. She was doing her best to stay clean; I knew it.

Meanwhile things at Mrs. Houston's house were getting worse, as the sexual assault was a frequent thing now. I finally worked up the courage to tell Mrs. Houston what was happening. Her response was not what I expected; in fact, she didn't respond at all. When I finished, she asked me if that was all and then left the room. I remember sitting there thinking that she would come right back and tell me that everything would be okay, that she was here to protect me and that I was not alone. She never did.

I thought that at least her nephew would stop coming around, but he didn't. He still babysat me, and he still, sexually abused me. In fact, anytime the family got together I felt tension from the other family members, but no one ever talked to me about my sexual abuse. I could feel them staring at me and I heard whispers, but no one ever asked me if I was okay or talked to me about what was happening.

One day we were having a cookout; we were at my perpetrator's house, just a few doors up from Mrs. Houston's home. I left the cookout and walked to Mrs. Houston's house alone. I shut myself in the bathroom and cried. Although I didn't have the words for it at the time, I was experiencing victim blaming. We grow up as children with the understanding that adults keep us safe. I had shared with Mrs. Houston that I was sexually abused because I thought she would protect me. Not only did she not protect me, but I felt like I was the one to blame for the trauma I had experienced.

Ms. Sally was still present in my life as my caseworker. I don't know why I never told her about the sexual assault. I honestly didn't think that telling her, or any other adult for that matter, was an option. Maybe I had concluded that all the adults in my life would react the way that Mrs. Houston's family had reacted to my news.

The difficulty of experiencing trauma as a child is that you are fully aware that something is not right, but you don't have the ability to put those feelings into words. For me it took years to truly start unpacking the things that I experienced as a child and to put into words how those things made me feel. In some ways, I'm still very much going through that process. It's part of the healing journey, and it's never too late to begin. Over the years, I've learned a few techniques that have helped me to heal from my childhood trauma. I have written letters to the former me, that innocent little girl who had been taken from her mother, raped, and abused. In those letters, I speak to the child in me. I let her know that despite all the things she is experiencing, she will be okay. I let her know that she isn't alone, and even in those horrible moments that she experienced, God is still with her. I tell her that she grows up to be an amazing, resilient, and fearless woman. I tell her that one day she will look back on these situations and be so proud of herself that she overcame the things that were meant to break her.

Sometimes I speak directly to that little girl. When something triggers me and my mind goes back to her, I speak to her in the manner that I wish Mrs. Houston would have spoken to me. I became the adult that I needed back then. I comfort that little girl the way that I should have been comforted, and some days I weep and rock her to sleep the way she used to comfort herself as a child. There was nothing I could do for that little girl all those years ago, but now, I'm intentional and committed to helping her heal, even all these years later. She is me, and I am her.

In addition to the abuse at Mrs. Houston's house, Robin continued to do things and I continued to be blamed for them. Stealing food, hitting the other foster kids, hiding things, you name it. Robin would blame me and then take delight in watching me get punished for her actions. One day I came home from school; I walked home from the bus stop. As I got closer, I noticed that there was a fire truck in front of Mrs. Houston's house. I went in through the front door and found the fire fighters in the house. I walked through the living room and into the kitchen. The home was smoky and the firefighters walked past me as I walked into the home. I went into the kitchen and saw that the wall above the stove had been burnt all the way up to the ceiling. Mrs. Houston was sitting in the kitchen, I asked Mrs. Houston what happened, her response was that she had left something on the stove too long. She left it at that, and I didn't think anything else of it. I remember hearing Mrs. Houston on the phone saying that we would be going to stay at a hotel while things got cleaned up and fixed. As a young child, I was excited about staying at a hotel; it sounded like an adventure. I was so naive and innocent that I didn't really understand the full impact of what had happened. I also didn't realize that I would end up being blamed for starting that fire and other horrible events.

Shortly after that incident, the visits with my mother stopped. I had gotten used to spending Wednesdays with my mom and every other weekend. One Wednesday, I was excited and anxiously waiting for my case worker to pick me up and take me to visit my mom. She never came to pick me up. Weeks went by and I heard nothing; the visits had stopped, and no one provided me with an explanation.

Finally, several weeks later, I received a phone call from my caseworker. She told me that my mom had gone back to prison and had made the decision to put me up for adoption. I couldn't believe what I was hearing; I was devastated. My mind went back to all the conversations that I had with my mom about her fighting to keep me. My heart was crushed, and I felt like I was being abandoned all over again. I felt disappointed that my mother hadn't kept her promise of me moving back in with her. I was sad and mad at my mother. The feeling of rejection took over again, and I began to feel that nobody ever wanted me; this was a thought that would resonate with me for decades. I internalized her putting me up for adoption as never being good enough for anyone and everyone who I cared about would leave. Things had been looking up for my mother and I, handling the sexual abuse and the tension with the adults was easier because I had my mom, even though I was in my twenties before I ever told her about the abuse. Now, she was no longer there for me.

As if things couldn't get any worse, one day I came home from school and Mrs. Houston had me set my backpack in the living room. She asked me to come into the kitchen. She had a chair by the stove; this was the place where she would do my hair. I sat in that chair in the kitchen from the moment I got home until well into the evening. Mrs. Houston was putting braids into my hair. At this time Mrs. Houston had a newborn baby in her care, plus Robin and I. The baby was in a crib in the back of the house with Robin the entire time. I had gone to the back to use the restroom one time; other than that, I sat in the chair while my hair was being braided. While Mrs. Houston was braiding my hair, she would periodically stop to go and check on the baby and Robin. After a couple of hours, she went to the back of the house, and I heard a scream. She ran from out of the back of the house, grabbed the phone and ran back to the room where the baby and Robin were. I didn't know what was going on. The police arrived and it was then that I found out that a plastic bag was in the baby's crib and that the baby was not breathing. I don't know if the baby survived, or what happened from there. I was taken out of Mrs. Houston's house and taken to another home that same evening.

The next morning, I was taken to what I believe was a counselor. At this point no one had given me much detail about what was going on. I remember the darkness of the room. It was dark and dingy. I remember a man with a white beard sitting at a desk. I walked into the room and sat down in a chair in front of the desk. The man asked me a series of questions. The entire time I sat there wondering why I was at this place, when I would get to leave, and why I was being asked so many questions. My world changed when the man with a white beard asked me why I had decided to set Mrs. Houston's house on fire, and why I had placed the plastic bag in the crib with the baby. What?! I wasn't present for both of those situations; I knew it, and Mrs. Houston knew it. I was so shocked and confused and a million questions began to run through my mind. Where was Mrs. Houston? I just needed her to come and clear all of this up. How did a misunderstanding like this happen? I've never ever been in trouble; certainly, they know I didn't do this.

The man with the white beard informed me that Mrs. Houston had reported to the state that I had both started the fire and placed the bag in the baby's crib. I was shocked and heartbroken. I could not believe what I was hearing. I tried to explain over and over, to tell my side of the story but no one would hear me or believe me. I couldn't believe that someone I trusted had betrayed me. I left the dark and dingy room and was taken immediately to a facility. No one took the time to explain to me what this place was or why I was there, or how long I would be there. No one cared enough to hear my side of the story, the truth. I was a child, so to them, my words were worthless. My mother had placed me for adoption, and now the woman I lived with for years had betrayed me. The pain cut deep, and no one seemed to care.

I was treated poorly from the moment I walked into that facility. To this day, no one has ever explained to me where I went. I assume now, as an adult, that it was a juvenile facility of some sort. I also never learned what happened to the baby that I was accused of harming. Everything was scheduled meals, group activities, bedtime, etc. The place felt like a prison except it was filled with pre-teens and teens, and I was the youngest child there. A couple of times a week I was forced to see counselors who were on staff in the facility. They continually accused me of setting the fire and placing the bag in the baby's crib. To make matters worse, it seemed that their main objective was to force me to confess to these things.

(TW): suicide and sexual violence

When I first got there, I told anyone and everyone I could that I didn't belong there. I tried to tell my story repeatedly but still it fell on deaf ears. I tried repeatedly to tell the staff that I didn't belong there, and that there had been a mistake. Nobody believed me, and nobody would explain to me what was happening. I became depressed, and I couldn't understand why no one believed me. I couldn't understand why I was treated like a criminal when I knew I did nothing wrong. I couldn't understand why or how this was my life. So, I simply stopped talking. I would sit in my counseling sessions and just stare at the counselor when they asked questions. I became consumed with the thought of dying because death had to be better than my life at the time. Death felt like the only way out. I tried for the first time in my life to commit suicide.

There were older boys in the facility with me and they made no attempts to separate them from me. There was a teenage boy whose room was across the hall from mine. He would make inappropriate comments to me that I wasn't old enough to understand, yet I knew that they made me feel uncomfortable. I would tell the staff, but no one seemed to care. In their minds, I was some hardened criminal and they treated me as such. As a result, yet again I became victim to sexual abuse and rape.

(TW-End)

Holidays in this place would come and go like regular days. One Christmas I remembered all the children gathering around the tree and opening gifts. For a moment, I got excited about the possibility of seeing what was under the tree for me. All I ended up getting was an orange. A single orange. I'm assuming the other children had family members who brought them gifts. I had no one. So now, in addition to feeling rejected, trauma left me feeling depressed and suicidal. I was living with a label and defending myself against things that I never did anything to deserve. Although my suicide attempt failed, I experienced a form of death in that place. My childhood died in that place.

Most of my childhood and time spent in that horrible place is a blur. I've learned through counseling that my brain learned to block certain memories as a defense mechanism. The process is called trauma-related dissociation. When we experience trauma and cannot physically escape, our minds find a way to mentally escape. There are many symptoms of trauma-related dissociation, but my symptoms manifested through something called Dissociative Amnesia. Dissociative Amnesia is caused by our emotions and memories not being able to fully connect due to the trauma we have experienced. While I have memories from my childhood, there are many things that I don't remember.

When it was time to leave that place, a new social worker picked me up; her name was Bernice Bell. She was dark-skinned, slim, and beautiful, and her lipstick was always on point. I was scared. I didn't know what was going to happen and I literally hadn't spoken to anyone in months. Mrs. Bernice was nice; her spirit was calming. As she drove me away from that horrible place, I remember looking out the window and seeing the grass for what felt like the first time ever. It was so vibrant, so green, and so alive. It was the opposite of the darkness that surrounded me. I stared at the sky and how blue it was. It was then that I realized that I hadn't seen life outside of the facility the entire time that I was there. It was as if somehow, I had forgotten that outside existed.

I hadn't said one word to Mrs. Bernice. She must have sensed my fear because she started talking to me. What she said to me changed my entire life in one moment. She reached over and placed her hand on my knee, and she said to me, "I know what you've been through, and I know you didn't do this. Everything will be okay now. I believe you." I cry every time I think of this moment, and even as I sit here writing this, tears are falling uncontrollably from my eyes. I had spent years trying to explain my innocence to people. I cried; I declared my innocence with everything in me until I literally had no more words to express. No one would listen, and no one believed me. Here I am, with a woman who had only met me less than an hour prior and to whom I hadn't spoken a word, and she knew; she knew!

It doesn't matter what other people say or believe about you. God's belief in you overshadows anything anyone else thinks about you. The people whom God intends to be in your life, the people who are part of your destiny, won't need to be convinced of who you are. You won't have to beg them to see you or believe you. They will see your heart. That day, I didn't have to say anything to Mrs. Bernice. She saw my heart and God had placed her in my life for that very moment. She was God's way of letting me know that He had not forsaken me or forgotten me. For the first time in my life, I envisioned a positive future for myself. To this day, I don't think that Mrs. Bernice knows the impact that she made on my young eleven-year-old life. God is with us, even in the darkest of moments. We don't always feel Him, especially when we are so overcome with the happenings of life. But in the same way that the green grass and the blue sky made me feel after so long, that's how God's presence shows up when we least expect it.

Upon leaving the facility, Mrs. Bernice took me to the home of Mrs. Johnson. Mrs. Johnson* lived in Alorton, Illinois. She was widowed and had recently had a sixteen-year-old foster girl in her care who had run away. Due to that, Mrs. Johnson was very strict. I was not allowed to go anywhere, couldn't have any friends over, and had to always remain in her sight. Mrs. Johnson had a sweet side, but she was also verbally abusive and sometimes physically abusive. I was still quiet and reserved, and I think that my calm temperament disturbed her. I've noticed that this is something that seems to bother people from time to time. Like, why are others disturbed by peace? The fact is that sometimes the God in us irritates the demon(s) in them.

During my time at Mrs. Johnson's house, I attended Neeley Elementary school, in East Saint Louis, Illinois. On top of my quiet, calm demeanor, I also had what was referred to as a "lazy eye." The term is Dissociated Vertical Deviation (DVD) which is characterized by a slow, upward drift of one eye when the other is fixated on an object. Essentially, I would be looking at something, and one eye would be focused while the other one would be drifting. People were confused about what I was focusing on. My voice has always been deep and while growing up, the kids would make fun of it, calling me a man. I can even remember a girl making fun of my toes because they were "freaky long." As far as others were concerned, it seemed that everything was wrong with me. I now know much differently. To make matters worse, Mrs. Johnson also insisted on making me wear the styles of clothes that she, or maybe even her mother had worn when they were my age. I was relentlessly bullied by kids.

The persistent bullying combined with the rejection, depression, suicidal thoughts, and the trauma of being locked in that facility made my childhood very difficult. Not to mention, no one talked to me about my experiences in the facility. No one explained it. It happened to me, and I was left to make sense of it at the age of eleven. I had been prescribed Prozac for depression. I was seeing a counselor regularly and trying to learn how to process life. Then puberty started. While I had absolutely no self-esteem in myself, I was viewed as a threat by girls my age whose boyfriends had started to notice my, uh... well... early development, particularly in the chest area. Girls would start fights with me in the hallways and insist that I "meet them at the flagpole" after school. It was usually always over some snotty-faced, pre- teen boy, with bad breath that I had no interest in at all and who I could beat up if needed. However, the kids and peer pressure were relentless. Once an invite to the flagpole had been extended, there was no escaping it. I would show up at the flagpole and give it my best shot. Sometimes I won, and sometimes I lost.

The fights would usually result in suspension from school and Mrs. Johnson did not play. She would make me pick my own switch from the tree for my whooping's. One day I got suspended from school and decided that I wouldn't tell Mrs. Johnson. I spent the evening running to the phone every time it rang hoping to answer the phone call from the school before she could get to it. I answered the call from the school, did my best Mrs. Johnson impersonation and hung up the phone feeling confident that Mrs. Johnson would never know that I had been suspended again. I showed up to school the next day, walked into my classroom as if nothing was wrong and took my seat. In less than five minutes I was pulled out of class and sent back to the principal's office. When Mrs. Johnson had to leave work and come to pick me up from school, I received the worst whooping of my life. I think my ass is still sore from that experience.

| three |

Family MATTERS

I desired a family more than anything else in life. I remember watching other kids my age with their families and daydreaming what it would be like to have a home with a mom and a dad. I had an extensive collection of McDonald's Happy Meal toys, and I would spend hours in my room building homes and creating families with the Happy Meal toys. I discovered a love for board games at a young age, but since I was an only child at Mrs. Johnson's house, I learned to play board games on my own. I desperately wanted a family to do family things with. Not only did I want to belong, but I also needed to belong. Yet, I was too afraid to even begin the process of forming relationships. Any friends that I had didn't come from my efforts. They were usually formed out of convenience. That's how my friendship with Ida* occurred.

Ida lived across the street from Mrs. Johnson's house. She was the only person whose home I was allowed to visit under Mrs. Johnson's strict rules, so I spent a lot of time with her. We watched movies and listened to music. Tupac was a favorite of ours. In fact, we were waiting at the bus stop when we heard that Tupac had died. We cried as if a close family member had died. I considered Ida my best friend, and I even grew connected to her family.

One day, we were waiting for the school bus. Ida and I were chatting away as usual. She seemed normal, and I had no indication that anything was wrong. The bus arrived and she asked me to sit in the back of the bus with her. I believed this girl was my friend, so I had no hesitation in following her to the back of the bus. A few minutes later Ida looked at me and then swung at my face. Suddenly, I felt my face sting and I could feel something running down my face, it was blood. Ida had taken a razor blade and slashed me across the face with it because my face, in her words, "was too pretty." Thankfully, the razor didn't cut too deep, and the only physical mark left is a cut that's about an inch long on the bridge of my nose. This incident caused me to withdraw from everyone. I felt betrayed yet again. The worst part of the situation was that I lost the only real friend I had, and I felt lonely.

Loneliness was an ever-present factor in my life. I didn't realize it then, but loneliness would become the theme in my life that taught me how to rely on God, and God alone. We are never truly alone; God is always there. I experienced God for the first time at Mrs. Johnson's house. I remember sitting in my room and talking out loud, expressing my feelings. I had never been to church at this point, but I always felt an indescribable presence in my life. On this day I decided that I would speak to this presence. I was so sad and depressed; I began to talk to this presence and pour my heart out. Suddenly, I felt arms wrap around me. I looked down and couldn't see anything with my visual eyes, but the arms were there; I could feel them. For what felt like the first time in my life, I felt peace. The feeling was so unfamiliar to me that it terrified me - yet it was so comforting at the same time. I had no idea what I had just experi-enced. I knew then that despite my circumstances of not having a family, being abused, and betrayed, I wasn't alone. Years later, after

I began attending church consistently, I felt that same presence. It was only then that I understood just how much God had been there for me the entire time.

All the pain that I had experienced up to that point had a purpose. What I realize now is that some of us have a mark on us. Not a physical mark, but it's an undeniable marking, one that makes us stand out to others. No matter how hard I tried to blend in with the crowd and to keep myself out of the spotlight, I couldn't. No matter how hard I wanted to go through life unnoticed, I couldn't. I was marked and visible to others whether I wanted to be or not, and that marking is called an anointing. An anointing is the undeniable mark of God on a person's life. It's a mark that isn't visible with the natural eye, but it is detected in a person's spirit. It's the evidence of God's clear presence in their lives. Sometimes others recognize it in us before we do, and the anointing attracts jealousy.

Unfortunately, some of us never realize the anointing that we have in our lives. It's there, but we allow the things that we experience to become the focus and the measurement of who we are as individuals. We spend so much time victimizing the experiences of our lives that we don't ever come out on the other side of those experiences. That's where we meet the anointing; It's on the other side of the victimization. When we get stuck in victimization, we don't realize that we are mistreated not because there is something wrong with us, but because there is something so right about us.

Despite Satan's efforts, the anointing cannot be stopped. Satan is on a mission to keep us from recognizing it and most definitely from achieving its goals. As a result, those who are anointed usually experience complicated, unexplainable life experiences. The good news is that not even trauma can take away our anointing.

Jeremiah 17:8 (NIV) states, "They will be like a tree planted by the water that sends out its roots by the stream. It does not fear when heat comes: its leaves are always green. It has no worries in a year of drought and never fails to bear fruit."

You can't stop the anointed!

This revelation was a game changer. I no longer apologize for being me and I don't operate from a place of shame. There was never anything wrong with me. The problem was never with me. I am who I am simply because God saw fit to anoint my life. That's it; that's the only reason. This revelation didn't happen overnight; it has been a process to understand this.

It wasn't until a few years ago, during a conversation with a close friend of mine, Sha'Neka Daniels, that I realized the anointing that God had placed on my life. Sha'Neka and I were discussing a situation I was experiencing with someone who I considered to be a friend. This person had turned on me without explanation and I was really struggling to understand why. I started talking to Sha'Neka about this situation, and about feeling like I didn't fit in with others and I was constantly misunderstood. Sha'Neka stopped me mid-sentence and said, "Sis, you don't fit in because you're not meant to fit in!"

She explained to me that God had destined me for greater purposes and that I was meant to stand out. She explained that the people that were meant to understand me would, but there would be those who would envy the things that made me different. She then played a song for me, sung by Fantasia Barrino called "Necessary." The lyrics to the song are very simple, but very powerful. *"I am who I am today because God used my mistakes. He worked them for my good, like no one else ever could... it was necessary."* Sha'Neka has since passed away, but I will reference her a lot in this book because her presence in my life was truly God-ordained. She was one of those people in my life who just saw me for me, and no explanation was needed. Ever.

I ended up staying with Mrs. Johnson for several years. It was the closest experience to having a family that I had ever had. Mrs. Johnson was a sweet lady for the most part, but she had a mean streak. At times, she would become verbally abusive and tell me things like I would never be anything more than what my mother was. I would often hear Mrs. Johnson talking about me to her children or other adults and saying negative things about me. I did my best to tune those things out but even now, I still feel the impact of some of the things that she said to me. I began to believe some of those things and the depression began to sink in even more.

It was made clear to me by my social worker that my stay at Mrs. Johnson's house would be over soon, as she was older, and her health had started to decline. In foster care, they try to prevent the children from aging out of the system (turning eighteen) without being adopted. The closer I got to that age, the more urgency they placed on my adoption. I was featured on the local news as part of a segment that highlighted older foster care children who were up for adoption. I was also given the option to decide who would adopt me. I had frequent meetings with "potential parents" but although I desired a family more than anything, I turned down those families. There was one potential family who I particularly remember. I met them at their church for our initial meeting. They were Seventh Day Adventists; I know that because I remember how weird it felt to go to church on a Saturday. This family had a son. After church I went with the family and the only thing that I remember is the way the son looked at me. I felt uncomfortable and it reminded me of the sexual abuse that I had already experienced in my life. After the visit, when my social worker asked me if I would be interested in being adopted by that family, I told her no. I remember her being confused because I never fully explained why; I simply told her that I wasn't interested.

Although I still hadn't found my adoptive family, I was in communication with some of my birth family. I am the baby of my birth family. I knew I had two older sisters, and because they are older than me, they were able to stay with my grandmother. I was considered too young to stay with my grandmother, so I ended up in foster care. During my stay with Mrs. Johnson, I was allowed to go and visit my sisters and my grandma. My sisters were teenagers and I looked up to them so much. They both had this independence about them that inspired me. They had been through a lot and yet, they were my protectors.

My earliest memory of my sisters involved celebrating a birthday. I later found out when I recited this memory to my sisters that it was my oldest sister's birthday. We were at my grandma's house; I remember a white cake sitting on the table. I was very young. My mother came and took me on a walk. We walked down the street from my grandma's house and walked into another home. There were a lot of people in this home, and I remember a strong smell of something burning, like plastic. My mother took me down into the basement, and there were glass bottles all over the top of a counter, and the basement was dark and dingy. She sat me in a big recliner, and then she disappeared. I was surrounded by strangers and screaming at the top of my lungs. I sat there and cried for what seemed like a long time. Finally, one of my sisters walked into the house. She was mad and she was yelling for my mother. She picked me up and took me out of that home. She saved me, and I felt protected. I now know that my mother had taken me to a crack house and had me around complete strangers while she went and got high.

In addition to regularly visiting my sisters and grandma, I also participated in a program for foster care kids. The program was part of Southern Illinois University Edwardsville (S.I.U.E). Since Mrs. Johnson was so protective and strict, my interaction with other children was very limited. There were no play dates with other children, and outside of Ida who lived across the street, I had no friends. The S.I.U.E program gave me an escape; it was something to look forward to. We would watch movies, go to the skating rink, have parties and all kinds of fun activities. The best part about the program was that the kids were foster kids like me, and I made friends.

I ran into Mrs. Houston once, the lady who had accused me of setting the fire and placing the bag in the baby's crib, at a banquet for foster children when I was living with Mrs. Johnson. She approached me and acknowledged that she had lied by telling the state that I was the one who set the fire and placed the bag in the crib. She then proceeded to tell me that she had another child that reminded her of me and made her miss me. She then had the nerve to ask me if I "wanted to come back home." She told me that she knew I wasn't at fault, but that she couldn't' admit that Robin (the other foster child who constantly did things and blamed them on me) had done those things because she "couldn't afford to lose the income that Robin provided." I guess that due to Robin's "disabilities" Mrs. Houston was paid more to care for Robin. On top of all of that, Mrs. Houston asked me for a hug. I stood there and stared at her speechlessly. The woman who was responsible for so much of the trauma I had experienced was sitting here admitting fault as if she was talking to me about what she had eaten for breakfast!

She clearly had no remorse for her actions and had no concern for how her actions had impacted me. I hate to think of what other foster care children experienced under Mrs. Houston's care. I have replayed that conversation so many times in my head, with all the things I should have said and how I should have responded. I replayed this conversation with Mrs. Bernice and with my therapist. I'm not sure if Mrs. Houston was ever confronted about this conversation or held accountable for her lies. I also never got the apology that I deserved. I had to make the choice to forgive her anyway. It is a hard task to forgive someone for hurting you so badly, especially when they have no remorse. I didn't forgive Mrs. Houston for her sake; she will answer to God for her actions. I forgave her for my sake, because I didn't want the burden of carrying that much hate for someone for the rest of my life. This woman had taken so much from my past already, I would be damned if I let her take my future too. I had control over that, and I refused to let her have it.

In writing this book, I recently researched Mrs. Houston, all the way down to Google mapping her home. It still looks the same, only less grandiose than I remember. I learned that she is still alive, in fact, my sister knows exactly who she is and would see her from time to time in town. Mrs. Houston, you know who you are, despite the pseudonym I have given you in this book. You know. I forgive you. I pray that this book finds you so that you can see God's greatness. What you meant for evil, God turned it around for good. God gets the victory in my story, despite your efforts. May God have mercy on your soul.

I moved around from foster home to foster home, most of the time with little or no notice. Such a lack of stability can cause a person to feel unwanted. Additionally, it created an ideology that everyone I loved, I would lose. I became afraid to get too close to anyone because I just knew that it would only be a matter of time before they would leave my life. Unfortunately, this theory proved to be true most of the time. We have all heard the statement that there is power in our words, but it goes a step beyond that: there is power in our thoughts too. What we think about ourselves, and about life in general, has a way of manifesting.

By entertaining the thought that anyone I loved would leave, it left me feeling alone in this world. I learned to protect myself by not allowing myself to get close to anyone. I became withdrawn and secluded. I rarely spoke to anyone, didn't bother making friends in school, and I didn't care much about anything because in my mind, it was all temporary anyway. This mentality stayed with me throughout my childhood and well into adulthood. I still had a great desire for a family.

I was still receiving monthly visits from my social worker Mrs. Bernice. Her visits usually ended with her asking me if there was anything she could do for me. On one visit I responded to that question by asking her if she knew if I had any other biological siblings. She responded that she would investigate and get back to me. The next month, Mrs. Bernice returned. She informed me that she had done some research and discovered that I had an older brother who was adopted as an infant. He was adopted into a family in Utah. Mrs. Bernice had reached out to the family, and they were interested in meeting me.

I had been at Mrs. Johnson's house for a few years by that time, and Mrs. Johnson's health had started to decline. Her niece came to live with us along with her toddler son. One night we were all awakened by a loud thud. We discovered that Mrs. Johnson had suffered a stroke in the middle of the night, and it had caused her to fall out of the bed. An ambulance came and took Mrs. Johnson to the hospital, and she didn't return home for several weeks. When she returned, she no longer had the ability to speak. I remember feeling relieved that Mrs. Johnson could no longer speak, which meant that she could no longer hurl the insults and abuse that she had used to attack me previously. As awful as that thought was, it was my truth; I was relieved. However, what was happening to Mrs. Johnson was sad, and I hated to see her experience the effects of a stroke.

Things were never the same when Mrs. Johnson returned, as her health had gotten worse, and I knew it was only a matter of time before I would be sent to a new home. I had been communicating with the family that had adopted my brother in Utah. I spoke to them on the phone a few times and had received letters from them and all the other kids they had adopted, including my biological brother. Visits with my grandmother and sisters had stopped. Finally, the call came that I would be going to another family.

The Smith* family lived across the street from a corner store where gang members hung out. They had bullets in the side of the house from drive-by shootings that had taken place. Once it got dark outside, we couldn't sit in the living room, which was located upstairs and directly across from the corner store. Let's just say, the block was hot. During the day I would sit outside on the porch and just observe. I saw drug deal after drug deal, I saw prostitutes, I saw fights; you name it. One time a Caucasian man, clearly lost, pulled up to the stop sign in a red car. One of the gang members approached his car and motioned for him to roll down his window. This poor guy, clearly lost, rolled his window down while smiling and seemingly excited to talk. I watched as the gang member asked him what he was doing around and here and if he was lost. I then watched as he pulled his arm back and then I heard a loud "pop." He had punched the Caucasian guy in his face. The little red car took off so fast and I remember thinking that the driver would probably never be the same after that encounter.

One day, while driving home from church, a male cousin of the Smith family was sitting next to me in the car. He started rubbing my leg inappropriately, right there in front of everyone, I called him out and told him to not touch me like that. The looks he received from everyone else in the car were very telling. I would have hated to be a part of the conversations that took place as a result. For the first time in my life, I had spoken up for myself. The shy little girl who had endured so much sexual abuse had found her voice!

Shortly after I moved to the Smiths' house, I was informed by my social worker that my grandmother had passed away several months earlier. This was the reason why the visits with my sisters had stopped. Not only was I not notified that she was gone, but I didn't even get a chance to attend her funeral. To make matters worse, since my sisters were older, they had moved, and my social worker couldn't tell me where they were. I had lost my only contact with my birth family, and I was devastated.

I was still in contact with my birth brother's adopted family, and they were interested in adopting me. It was decided that I would travel to Utah and stay for a month, and from there it would be my decision on whether I stayed. I had never heard of Utah before, and when I asked around about it all I heard were stories about the Mormons. I heard things about them such as they had horns and believed in having multiple wives. The rumors about the religion were so intense that even Mrs. Bernice, who was still my social worker, was very nervous about my trip to Utah. She insisted on traveling with me and staying a few days with me in Utah to "check things out."

| four |

The "Perfect Life"

Mrs. Bernice and I arrived in Utah. The Hadley family picked us up from the airport. The first thing I noticed upon my arrival to Utah were the mountains. I arrived in the summer, so they were green and surrounded by clouds. They were so beautiful, but they intimidated me immediately. The mountains were not only tall, but they were visible in every single direction you looked. I was stepping into an unknown environment; everything about the situation was new and scary. I knew that at the end of the month-long stay I could leave if I decided, but the mountains made me feel trapped; they made me feel that the decision to stay here was final. They made me feel hopeless. There was something about not being able to see anything beyond the mountains that felt final for me.

We approach a lot of our life situations in the same manner that I approached my first encounter with mountains. I had spent my entire life beyond the mountains, yet here in this new scary situation, the mountains felt like the end for me. How many times do we face mountains, or challenges in our lives, and think that it's the end for us? We may have dealt with bigger challenges in the past, maybe even the same challenge as the one we are facing.

God brought us through the previous challenges, and logically we know that He hasn't failed us; yet here we sit, staring the current "mountains" in the face and feeling defeated. It's as if we had never overcome anything before. I was a survivor, and God had a flawless track record of bringing me through, but yet *this* felt final for me (insert palm to the face)!?

To say that Utah was an adjustment would be an understatement. Everyone was Caucasian, and in the part of town that the Hadley's lived in, everyone was Mormon. After meeting a few of the neighbors, I was quickly able to lay the "Mormons have horns" rumors to rest. I was relieved that the structure of their heads looked normal, for the most part. Mrs. Bernice had questions about the Mormon faith, I mean QUESTIONS. She must have grilled the Hadley's for hours about their beliefs. After a couple of days, she left Utah but not before making sure I knew that I didn't have to go along with any religion that I didn't feel comfortable following. I did my research and deep dived into the Mormon religion. I had questions, and quickly discovered that no one could answer those questions. Eventually, I decided that the Mormon religion was not for me, for various reasons.

Meeting Quinton, my biological brother, for the first time, was awkward. We had similarities in the way we looked, yet we knew very little to nothing about each other. Quinton was a typical big brother; he annoyed me a lot. We had a lot of fighting initially, but I wasn't innocent in the matter. One day Quinton made me so mad that I threw a metal folding chair at him and proceeded to chase him around the house. Looking back, I understand what a terrible move that was. What could I say… at that time I may have been removed from the 'hood, but the 'hood was very much a part of me. Growing up in foster care, I had seen a lot. I had built a lot of defense mechanisms to protect me from the pain that I had experienced.

For me, fighting was one way. I would never start a fight, but I would defend myself if needed. I had learned from all of those "meet me at the flagpole" invitations I received. In complete transparency, my temper has calmed down a lot, and most people would probably never know that I had that side to me. My relationship with God has helped tremendously. I work on controlling my emotions daily, but in the words of a great songwriter, "Try Jesus, but don't try me, because I throw hands." No matter how close to God I get, I'm afraid that that statement will never NOT apply to me.

As we neared the end of my thirty-day stay in Utah, I knew I had to decide about staying in Utah or returning to foster care in Illinois. Truthfully, I had experienced such a culture shock coming here that I didn't know if I wanted to stay. I had never been around so many white people in my life. Things were so different, and I just didn't think I could be happy here. One day after another bad fight with Quinton, I grabbed my suitcase and started packing. I had had enough, and I was getting out of this place. I wasn't going to stay another day dealing with this annoying older brother of mine in this weird place.

In the middle of me packing the few belongings I had, Quinton came into the room and started crying. He looked at me and said, "Please don't leave, you're all I have." Suddenly it hit me, while I had been around our birth family, and had the opportunity to know them, he never had that opportunity. He was adopted before he turned two years old. I was his connection to this other portion of his life and honestly, his identity. I knew then that despite how I felt, I needed to stay. I'm sure that if Quinton reads this book, he won't get this far into the book. Don't tell him I told y'all about him crying.

Most people adopt Black children, or children from other races, with the best intentions. They see an opportunity to help by creating a good environment for these children. They bring the children into their respective homes and for the most part, they expect those children to blend into their culture, not realizing that they have a culture of their own that they will eventually yearn to know. They don't even need to be exposed to their culture to desire it. It's ingrained in their being; it is in their roots. Despite their best efforts, the child is done a great disservice by being completely removed from their culture. There is a level of trauma that they experience, almost identical to that of an identity crisis.

I was fortunate to serve on the board and volunteer for a nonprofit that works with children of color to help educate, empower, and encourage children of color. It's called CurlyMe! Many of the families that participate in this nonprofit have adopted children from other races. I have a lot of respect for these parents because they recognize that even though they are bringing these children into their homes, they need to be allowed the opportunity to immerse themselves into their own culture. I'm happy to see these types of resources available because I have personally witnessed how my older brother has struggled with truly understanding his identity.

So here I was in Utah: new culture, new state, and a whole lot of uncertainty. To put it plainly, I hated it. The culture was different, and at this point in my life the mountains still made me feel trapped. I felt like I stuck out like a sore thumb. I knew that if I was going to be here, I needed to make the most of my life. I had planned on my life turning out much differently, and I found myself facing another crossroad. I could either let my circumstances control me or make the most out of the cards I had been dealt. I chose the latter.

I did my best to get involved in the community here. Unfortunately, I wasn't into many of the things that were considered "fun" in Utah. One of those things happened to be hiking. Shortly after my arrival in Utah, I inquired about what they did for fun here. That question resulted in me attempting to hike for the first time.

At this point, I wasn't even acclimated to the elevation change in the valley, but I also didn't even understand what elevation change was. I was taken to hike Mount Timpanogos which happens to be one of the top ten highest mountains in the state, at an elevation of almost 11,800 feet and is only 15 miles.... Needless to say, that hike didn't go well, and immediately I lost interest in any future hiking endeavors.

At this point, I knew that the Mormon church wasn't for me, but I also knew that my soul was searching for something, I felt incomplete, and I felt like my life needed something more. I had experienced the presence of God before I even knew His name and I wanted that again. I had yet to find it here in Utah, until I met Donald.

Donald and I met at a Utah night club. He was the first person to introduce me to a Baptist church. On my first visit there, I found the presence of God that I had longed for. A few months after I started attending that church, I accepted Christ into my life, and I was baptized. I was so excited to finally put a name to the presence that I had experienced as a young child. I started attending a new members' class and I couldn't get enough of learning and reading God's Word. I was nineteen years old at the time, I had my own apartment and was working full time, but I was broke. I purchased my first Bible from a dollar store. I was so excited to have it that the quality wasn't even important to me. I had questions, and for the first time in my life, those questions were being answered.

I was happy and completely satisfied with my dollar store Bible. I took it to Sunday School where I would highlight it and take notes. After a few weeks of this, one of the ladies in my Sunday School class presented me with a brand-new Bible that happened to be in my favorite color, purple. That lady was a blessing to me that day. I don't remember her name and since I've always been awkward when it comes to accepting gifts, I don't think that I thanked her properly or told her how much that meant to me. If this book happens to fall into her hands one day, thank you for contributing to the feeding and nourishment of a soul that was so desperate to find God. Sixteen years later, I still have and use that Bible.

Donald and I dated for four years, and we were married in August 2009. We continued to attend church together, and we served in the church together. My relationship with God began to grow stronger. I started to develop a relationship that became personal; it was beyond the presence that I had experienced all those years ago. I'm thankful for the opportunity that I took to get to know God on a deeper level, because unbeknownst to me, I was about to experience one of the greatest joys of my life while also living through my worst nightmare.

Shortly after our wedding, Donald and I learned that I was pregnant. On August 7, 2010, one day shy of our first wedding anniversary, Desirae Anita Brown was born. Her due date was a week earlier, on my birthday July 31st. By the time I was a week past due I was so anxious to give birth. I read online about all the ways that you could induce labor and I tried all of them. Well, almost all of them; one of the suggestions was to drink castor oil. After one sniff of the stuff, I knew that wasn't going to be the path for me. Instead, I decided to do a lot of walking. I loved shopping and needed a big area to walk in, preferably air conditioned, so I went to the mall. I walked around the mall for two hours. It worked, because my contractions started. Donald and I rushed to the hospital later that evening hoping that it was time. Instead, I received a shot of pain medicine in the behind and was sent home.

I continued to have contractions throughout the night, and the next day Donald had a basketball tournament and we still decided to go. We woke up, went to a breakfast spot, and then went to the basketball tournament. The contractions were progressing throughout the day, but the last thing I wanted to do was to sit at a hospital and wait. Instead, I sat at the basketball tournament. I was sitting next to Donald's sister. It was about 3:00 pm and by this time the contractions were so bad that I would stop my conversation with her mid-sentence, grab onto the back of the chair and squeeze as tight as I could while the contraction passed. By the time I asked Donald's sister to go and get Donald so we could go to the hospital, the contractions were nonstop.

That drive to the hospital was the longest drive of my life. The contractions were no joke. The pain was not only in my abdomen, but it radiated down my legs. I swear we hit every red light and stop sign possible. Finally, we pulled up to the hospital. We walked into the labor and delivery unit, and the receptionist asked, "How can we help you?" to which my response was, "I'm ready to have this baby, and if it's still not time, kill me now!" The nurses behind her said, "Yep, she's ready" and wheeled me away. The nurses discovered that I was *ready, ready* to have the baby when they realized I was already dilated to eight centimeters. They panicked and told me that I wouldn't be able to have any pain medicine. Once they popped my water, my labor stopped progressing. They ended up giving me an epidural, expecting that it would have time to kick in. It didn't. Next thing I knew, they were telling me to push. I felt every ounce of pain on my right side, as the epidural had only kicked in on the left side. After only twenty minutes of pushing, Desirae Anita Brown had made her entrance into the world, and just like her mother, she had done so in her way and on her own time.

Desirae had the sweetest temperament; she would look at me and just smile without being prompted. I loved having her in my arms and watching her do everything that babies do. Being in foster care, I strongly desired a family that looked like me, which is something that those who are raised with their birth families take for granted. I loved being a mom. I was absolutely in love with Desirae and everything that came with being a mom. Finally, I had the family I so strongly desired. I was living the "perfect life."

(TW): Death of a child

On January 6, 2011, when Desirae was one day shy of turning 5 months old, that all changed. I woke up to go to work that morning, I had just started working again after being a stay-at-home mom for the first few months. I worked during the day, and Donald worked during the night. I was in a rush that morning and ran over to kiss Desirae goodbye. As I bent down to kiss her, she gave me the biggest smile in the world. I kissed her several more times and told her how much I loved her. Work was a normal day; I was still in training at Qwest Communications, and I went about the morning as usual. A few minutes after 1:00 PM, while on lunch break, I had a bad feeling overcome me. I picked up my phone and called Donald, and it went straight to voicemail. I looked at the clock, it was 1:06 PM. I pushed the bad feeling to the side and went back to work.

Shortly after 3:00 pm, the President of the company came into our training room. He told me that I needed to come with him, that there were some visitors downstairs for me. We got into the elevator, and I asked him what was going on. He couldn't look at me, his response was, "It's not good." We got to the lobby of the building, and I was escorted into a conference room. When I walked in, there were about five or six people there - some police officers, and some social workers. They asked me to sit down. They informed me that my daughter, my joy, had died. I looked around at this group of people in disbelief, hoping that one of them would tell me that it all was a misunderstanding, and that Desirae was okay. Instead, I watched all of them just looking back at me. I realized that this wasn't a dream; this was reality. I felt my heart shatter. I wanted to say something. I wanted to ask questions, but all that came out of my mouth was a scream. This scream came from my most inner being, it was so strong and so powerful that it felt like the pieces of my newly shattered heart were flying out of my mouth like darts.

They put me in a white van and drove me home. It was around 4:00 pm in the afternoon and traffic was heavy. The ride home felt like it would never end, and when we finally arrived at my apartment, I walked in and was greeted by so many faces. There were three police officers there, my Pastor, Donald, and the social workers who had just brought me home. I remember feeling shocked; it felt like a dream then, and it still feels like a dream even now. They started asking me questions about my daughter, what she had eaten, if she was sick, etc. I asked them to stop asking me questions and asked to see my daughter. I had no interest in answering their questions. I wanted to see my baby.

I walked into the room that had been a place of joy, peace, and happiness just a few hours earlier, and saw my daughter, the child I carried for nine months and one week, my future, the one I had desired laying there lifeless. I rubbed my daughter's legs and kissed her. I told her I was sorry that I wasn't there and told her that I loved her so much. She passed away while she was sleeping, so in some ways, she just appeared to be sleeping. Then came time for them to take her body. In movies you see them remove a body in a body bag, I guess they don't make those for babies, so they asked me if there was a blanket that they could use to take her. They wrapped my angel in the blanket we had used for her baby blessing and carried her out of the apartment. I remember looking at Donald and seeing him so lost and heartbroken. I felt everyone looking at me, unsure of what to say or do. I didn't know what to do, but I knew I couldn't get through this on my own.

(TW): End

I wasn't sure that I would ever make it through this. The only thing I was certain of is that God was the only One who was going to pull me through. I knew then that I had a choice... allow this heartache and pain to overtake me, or trust in God and keep pushing forward. So, I asked the Lord to guide me, and I kept pushing forward. This was not a one-time decision and "everything worked itself out" kind of situation. This was something I continually had to decide to do, sometimes every minute, sometimes every hour, and sometimes every second. I kept saying under my breath, "Help me, Lord." I knew that my own personal strength could not get me through this, and I knew that Donald's strength in that moment couldn't get me through. I knew that the only person who could get me through this was the Lord. He was the only light I had in what is still the darkest moment of my life.

"I lift up my eyes to the mountains - where does my help come from? My help comes from the Lord, the Maker of heaven and earth." Psalm 121:1-2 NIV

That night was a whirlwind; everyone around me was on the phone replaying the details of Desirae's passing to someone who had just heard the news. There were people in and out of our two-bedroom apartment. Food started coming and the constant requests for me to sit down and eat something started. I was numb; I didn't know what to think or do. I was standing in the kitchen looking at a spread of food laid out, and the Pastor's wife walked over to me and said, "You know, it's okay to break down. You can be mad at God. You have every right to be." I understood the point she was trying to make, but I knew that if I allowed myself to go there, even for a moment, I may never return...

Eventually everyone left the house, and it was just Donald and me. I don't know when we fell asleep or how long we slept but I remember waking up and thinking that the day before was a nightmare and that Desirae was still alive. When I realized that the day before had really happened, it felt like I relived the moment all over again when I was informed of her passing. I was so overwhelmed with emotions that Donald and I decided that we would go for a walk to help ease our minds. We walked about a mile down the road, it was a cold winter day and we both had tears streaming down our faces. We were both in so much pain that we didn't know what to do with ourselves; we wanted relief from the pain, but we didn't know where to start.

We decided to go for a drive next. I remember watching the world around me; for everyone else it was a normal Thursday. I remember feeling angry that the world around me was moving on like nothing had ever happened when my entire world was crashing down. It was at that moment that I faced the choice again. Either allow this thing to rip me apart and become angry and bitter, or I could rely on the only help I knew. Now came the test, did I really believe in the Lord and Savior that I spoke so highly of? Did I really trust God as my Provider, my Savior, and my Friend? When things are foggy, unclear, and just plain unsteady, that's when God does His best work. That's when we hear Him the best, that's when, believe it or not, elevation can happen. Do you still say yes to God's will for your life even when it means living out your greatest nightmare? Even when it means warfare, pain, and difficulty? Does your yes *really* mean yes?

| **five** |

God, Is That You?!

Over the next couple of days, I had a roller coaster of emotions. One minute I was crying so hard that I felt as if my heart would stop beating. The next minute I was so calm that you wouldn't know that I was currently living my worst nightmare. It was during this time that I understood what the Bible meant when it said, "peace that passeth all understanding." I understood what it meant to be carried by the Lord.

"And the peace of God, which passeth all understanding, shall keep your hearts and minds through Christ Jesus." Philippians 4:7 KJV

"Yea though I walk through the valley of the shadow of death, I will fear no evil: for thou art with me; thy rod and thy staff they comfort me." Psalms 23:4

I was all the way in the valley of the shadow of death, but I knew that I wasn't alone. I could feel God with me every step of the way. As Christians we like to believe that our faith is strong; we go to church every Sunday proclaiming our love for God and talking about how merciful, kind, and gracious He is to us. We love the Lord with all our hearts and then the unthinkable happens. Is your relationship with the Lord strong enough to withstand the unthinkable? Mine wasn't, but I knew that the only way I would survive was by trusting God.

I planned the funeral, made all the arrangements, including picking out my daughter's casket. The funeral director informed me repeatedly that Desirae was taller than the normal "baby and toddler" caskets so they would have to bury her in a "child's" casket. Desirae's funeral came and went. The apartment suddenly felt bigger, and I was afraid of everything in it, as if the apartment had taken my daughter. Donald worked nights and went back to work after her funeral. I found it unbearable to be in the apartment alone. For about a month after Desirae's death, I would get off work, go to the apartment until shortly before dusk, drive thirty-five minutes to Pleasant Grove, sleep on my parents' couch until 3:30 am, wake up and drive back to Salt Lake City and arrive at the apartment just in time to meet Donald coming home from work - all because the thought of being alone was too unbearable.

I had experienced so much loss in my life, but the pain that I felt after Desirae's death was, and is, beyond comprehension. I had no idea how I would move forward, or if I was even capable of moving forward. I was living my absolute worst nightmare. I drew closer to God, and my relationship with Him went from surface-level to something deeper. Many people commented on my "remarkable strength" to keep living but the truth is, I was taking it day by day. I was barely holding on most days. I understood, on a deep level, how someone could turn to drugs and alcohol to "numb" their pain; it is only by the grace of God that I didn't seek pain relief through drugs and alcohol. I couldn't keep going because I was strong and had it all figured out; in fact, it was quite the opposite. I was able to keep going because I realized that I was completely broken and that only one Person could help me through this tragedy.

"Each time he said, "My grace is all you need. My power works best in weakness." So now I am glad to boast about my weaknesses, so that the power of Christ can work through me." 2 Corinthians 12:9 NLT

I realized that nothing or no one could provide me the help that I needed, so I changed my focus.

Donald and I both started serving more in our church as we both recognized that God was the source of our strength. For a while Desirae's death brought Donald and me closer; we had lived through something horrible and were both grieving in our own ways. Serving God and choosing to follow Him doesn't make us exempt from hardship. The more we serve, the closer we grow to God; the closer we grow to God, the more we start to walk in our God-given purpose. The more we walk in our God-given purpose, the more things in our lives shift.

Eventually Donald and I started growing apart. I never blamed him for Desirae's death; in fact, I was thankful that our daughter left this earth with her father right by her side. She wasn't alone, and that provided comfort to me. We did our best to recover our relationship, but we never fully bounced back.

Our divorce was finalized in April 2015. My entire life I desired nothing more than to have a family. I went from having a daughter and a husband, to finding myself completely alone again within a couple of years. I had everything I ever wanted given to me and then ripped away tragically. There I was again, faced with the choice again. I could become bitter, or I could trust in God.

Instead, I continued to make the decision to trust in God. Sometimes that was a day-by-day decision, and sometimes it was an hourly or a minute-by-minute decision. I knew at this point that trusting God was the right thing to do, but that didn't make it any easier. After all, I could argue that I had trusted God before and look where I was now. I knew that allowing myself to think this way would only harm me. So, no matter how I felt, I decided to keep pushing into God as Jehovah Jireh, no matter how little it made sense at the time. I had to guard my mind and protect my heart during this time. When negative thoughts would creep in, I had to find the strength to block them. Eventually those thoughts stopped forming. The mind is powerful; it is the gateway to everything we do. Our thoughts become our words; our words become our actions, and our actions become our habits. Always guard your mind and your heart.

As I became intentional about my relationship with God, things began to change for me. I began to crave God and His presence more. Bigger than that, I noticed the places in my life where His presence was absent. I was beginning to know God as Abba. The word Abba means Father in Hebrew. There is more to knowing God than just attending church, praying, and listening to worship songs -you know, the Christian basics.

Think of it as dating. I refer to the Christian basics as "dating" God. Yes, these things are the beginning of a relationship with God and are necessary to maintain a continued relationship with God, but they are just foundations and are meant to be built upon. There is purpose in dating, but it is not meant to be the end of a relationship. It is meant to be the beginning. The goal of dating is that eventually you take the relationship to a new level of commitment. You trust and depend on this person more because you are comfortable with them. You create routines with this person, and they become an integral part of your life. Our relationship with God works the same way. The goal is to stop dating God and to start a new level of commitment to Him. When you learn to trust and depend on Him for everything, to be completely surrendered to Him, you get to know Him as Abba.

On my journey to discovering God, not only did I begin to date God, but I also decided (foolishly) that I was ready for dating again.

I came to realize quickly that I was in over my head about dating and unrealistic about my views on marriage. I knew that since my divorce and Desirae's passing, God was trying to work on me. Satan knew it too, and true to his fashion, he set out to distract me and throw me off the path.

| six |

Sitting in My Own Mess

I realized that I had created an idol out of marriage. I was at a place in my life where I desired to be married more than I desired a relationship with God. The worst part of this realization was the fact that I didn't even notice that I had gotten to this level of desperation. The truth is, after my divorce, I had become a "serial monogamous dater." I was *ALWAYS* in a relationship, and often it was a serious relationship. I never dated multiple people at one time, and I was never one to entertain multiple sex partners. Instead, when one relationship would end, usually after a couple of years, I would end up right back into a new one a short time later.

The realization that I had made marriage an idol came with becoming self-aware. Growing closer to God requires us to have a sense of self-awareness. Self-awareness is being aware of our traits that make us who we are. This includes our positive and negative traits. Lacking self-awareness causes us to misunderstand ourselves, which can cause us to misunderstand God. A lack of self-awareness impacts our relationships, how we love ourselves, and how we love others. Self-awareness is different from self-esteem. Self-esteem involves your opinion of yourself, while self-awareness involves your ability to truly see yourself for who you are. Naturally, self-awareness can improve your self-esteem.

When we start to become more self-aware, a natural process starts where we learn to accept ourselves for who we are. When we learn to accept ourselves for who we are, we are more open to hearing what God says about us. The voices of self-doubt and insecurity will shrink, making room for the validations that Abba wants to pour into us. As our relationship with God increases, our love increases as well: love for God, love for others, and love for ourselves. I recognized that I lacked a genuine love for myself which made me desire to be in a relationship all the time. I began to search and ask myself, "So, what does God have to say about me?" I discovered the following:

"But the Lord said to Samuel, "Do not look on his appearance or on the height of his stature, because I have rejected him. For the Lord sees not as man sees: man looks on the outward appearance, but the Lord looks on the heart." 1 Samuel 16:7 ESV

"See how very much our Father loves us, for he calls us his children, and that is what we are! But the people who belong to this world don't recognize that we are

God's children because they don't know him." 1 John 3:1 NLT

"But you are a chosen race, a royal priesthood, a holy nation, a people for his own possession, that you may proclaim the excellencies of him who called you out of darkness into his marvelous light." 1 Peter 2:9 ESV

"For you formed my inward parts; you knitted me together in my mother's womb. I praise you, for I am fearfully and wonderfully made. Wonderful are your works; my soul knows it very well." Psalm 139:13-14 ESV

I learned that God says these things and so much more about us. I started to write down Bible verses about what God says about me.

I would post these verses on my bedroom mirror and read them often, but especially when doubt and insecurity started to creep in. When those negative thoughts would start to creep in, I had an arsenal full of Bible verses that I could use to attack those thoughts.

I quickly realized that preparing for marriage would require preparing myself, not for marriage, but for the real me. I discovered that at the core of my serial monogamy was the fear of being alone. The result was one dead-end relationship after another. The men I dated were not bad people, that was only by the grace of God, but for me they were marriage potential just for the sake of getting married.

In addition to self-awareness and learning to love, one of the main things that happens when you start to be intentional about your relationship with God, is that He starts revealing things to you. He often reveals these things through the Holy Spirit.

"But it was to us that God revealed these things by his Spirit. For his Spirit searches out everything and shows us God's deep secrets." 1 Corinthians 2:10 NLT

Growing closer to God, combined with getting to know the real me and sitting in my own mess, revealed to me how broken I truly was and started me on a path of healing and wholeness.

How often do we hear the phrase, "Be careful what you pray for" ...? We often pray for things at a surface level, forgetting or sometimes ignoring the steps that are required to have those prayers answered. Having already been married one time and desiring to be married again meant that I needed to be honest with myself about my shortcomings in my first marriage and take accountability. The divorce may not have been completely my fault, but it didn't mean that I didn't play a role in it. I knew that for full healing to take place, I needed to apologize to my ex-husband for the role that I played. I sent him a message on Facebook apologizing for the devastation of our marriage by acknowledging my role. There was peace and healing in that process.

The Holy Spirit is also referred to in the Bible as the spirit of truth.

"But when he, the Spirit of truth, comes, he will guide you into all the truth. He will not speak on his own; he will speak only what he hears, and he will tell you what is yet to come." John 16: 13 NIV

I am a living testament to this verse. When I tell you that through the Holy Spirit, I was forced to face the areas of my life where I had failed to be accountable. I was busy serving at church; I was the church clerk, deaconess, Sunday School teacher and a member of the youth choir. I was busy doing all the things that I thought would make God proud. I became overwhelmed and serving was no longer enjoyable. I realized that I was busy in the church, but I was busy doing absolutely nothing.

Yes, we should be serving; we should be working in our local church. It's important. However, when you take on too many tasks, you naturally become overwhelmed over time, and we miss important details. You stop focusing on the bigger picture and, if you aren't careful, you become ineffective. God gave us instructions on what we should do in life (Matthew 28:19-20) but He *never* said to run yourself ragged in the process. God Himself rested on the seventh day. I knew I needed to be intentional about my level of serving.

I began to ask God to show me His purpose for my life and I asked Him to guide my steps. Again, be careful what you pray for. The closer I got to God, my desire got stronger to live the way that He intended me to live. God kept drawing my attention to the verse, "Therefore go and make disciples of all nations, baptizing them in the name of the Father and of the Son and of the Holy Spirit," Matthew 28:19 NIV

This scripture is known as "The Great Commission" which is instruction from Jesus to spread the gospel throughout the world. Although I was "busy" in my church, I knew that I needed to shift my focus. I rededicated and recommitted my life to God. My daily prayer was "God, please place me where You would have me to be and allow me to do what is pleasing to you." Things in my life started changing, and not all the changes felt like they were for my good.

| seven |

The Wilderness Period

While I was on this newfound journey, I was forced to re-evaluate my surroundings. During this time, I had a "friend" reach out to me and tell me that she felt like we could no longer be friends, but she didn't know why. I was devastated. At the time, I very seldom allowed people to get close enough to me to consider them a friend. If I have ever called you a friend, a sister, or told you that I love you, I meant it from the bottom of my heart.

I may not have understood what was going on at the time, but in hindsight, I now understand that my new journey was changing me for the better. Not everyone would understand that change, because not everyone was meant to understand. Unfortunately, when people don't understand change, the natural tendency is to personalize it. We don't understand that it has nothing to do with us and everything to do with the other person. Our journey works just like the seasons do. People enter and exit our lives just like the seasons. They always serve a purpose in our lives, even if it's just for a moment. The journey requires us to let people go from time to time. The challenge is in trusting the process and learning to be okay with letting certain people go. Remember, it's not always about us.

This journey was going to require a lot from me, and more "letting go" than I was prepared for. I started to re-evaluate the church I was attending at the time. Matthew 28:19 kept replaying in my mind and I knew I needed to do more to spread the gospel in my little section of the world.

Although the church I was attending at the time was wonderful, and it had played such a vital role in the start of my journey to God, I noticed that the focus of the church was more on the existing members than it was on bringing new souls to God. The church should not just simply add new members, but it should create an environment that welcomes the unsaved to truly experience a relationship with God. As a result, I began to search for a church that was more in alignment with where I knew that God was directing me. For about three months, every Sunday, I traveled around Salt Lake County and visited different churches.

So here I was, walking completely by faith and venturing on a journey that made absolutely no sense to anyone else. I had people question my judgment, my character, and my relationship with God. That's the thing though, I wasn't looking for it to make sense to others; I was looking for it to make sense to me and to align with what God was directing me to do. This process was completely terrifying, and I thought about the many people in the Bible who also stepped out on faith and ventured out when it didn't make sense to others. I thought about Abraham and how close he came to sacrificing his son Isaac simply because he heard God telling Him to do it. I thought about Noah and the blind faith it took for him to build an ark on completely dry land, fill it with animals and travel for an undetermined amount of time. What kind of sense did that make at the time? How crazy did Noah look building this giant ark? And, if you would have told me that you needed me to find two of each animal and get it into the ark, you would have been disappointed. I don't know if you are understanding where I am coming from, but that would also include spiders and snakes!

This was unfamiliar territory to me. I felt completely alone and afraid. I lovingly refer to this period of my life as the "The Wilderness." We tend to fear what we don't understand. Being obedient to God often doesn't make sense because it's not meant to make sense. I heard the whispers from my "church family" about me looking for a new church because I wanted to sing on the praise team of another church. I heard the whispers of how I had lost my mind and was somehow so deep in sin that even I wasn't aware of it. I heard it all; it hurt, but I knew I had to keep moving.

Even now, writing this book, I have had people ask me about my being so reserved. They view me as someone who keeps people out intentionally, so how could I write an entire book on my life? This book is an act of obedience to God and my life story has been preserved for such a time as this. My life has never been my own; each life experience that I encountered has served a purpose, and that purpose was to bring glory to God's name. This book is not about me; it's about honoring God that through me, others may see God and His faithfulness to us.

"My old self has been crucified with Christ. It is no longer I who live, but Christ lives in me. So I live in this earthly body by trusting in the Son of God, who loved me and gave himself for me." Galatians 2:20 NLT

So here I am, being vulnerable and sharing my life story. It doesn't make sense, and there is *nothing* comfortable about this process, but I know that it's what God is requiring of me. So, I will choose to be obedient.

Following God and walking in His obedience is the absolute best thing that you can do in life. While the journey will be worth it, Jesus never hid the fact that following Him will cost you some things.

"And he said to all, "If anyone would come after me, let him deny himself and take up his cross daily and follow me. For whoever would save his life will lose it, but whoever loses his life for my sake will save it." Luke 9:23-24 (ESV)

Just like God provided help for those in the wilderness in the Bible, He also provided help for me. God sends exactly who we need when we need them. Angels truly do walk among us, and God assigns them to us. I had known Sha'Neka Daniels for years. We attended church together, helped on the dance ministry for a short time, and had been in each other's lives for quite some time. I had gotten Sha'Neka a job at the assisted living home where I was working, and when I decided to leave that job to help to open a new assisted living, Sha'Neka followed me to the new job.

We became close as we worked together, and at work, we were basically inseparable. Sha'Neka was a spiritual warrior. Although she was younger than me, she constantly encouraged me. When I lost "friends" and I struggled to understand why, she reminded me that not everyone was meant to go on my journey with me. When I made the choice to step out on faith and start looking for a new church home, she visited churches with me to make sure that I felt comfortable. We spent a lot of time talking about purpose.

Sha'Neka was an encourager, and every conversation that you had with her, you left feeling the need to go and pick up your Bible and spend time in the presence of God. I could be having the worst days and I would get a message from Sha'Neka with some sort of encouraging message. I still have all the text messages between Sha'Neka and me. One message that I still read often said, "Sis believe me when I say God will move things or people to get you in the position he needs you so that he can use you. It's no mistake that you are going through the things you are going through1 You may not see it now, but you have already started your ministry! God has been waiting for you to hear his voice. You are now following the path God wants you on. Look at the blessings that are already happening in your life." She pushed me through my wilderness when I didn't feel that I had the strength.

I continued to search for a new church home, and I narrowed it down to two amazing churches. Both churches were focused more on bringing salvation to unbelievers than they were with adding new members to their congregation. In fact, neither church really tracked who was considered a member of their congregation and who wasn't. On October 29, 2017, I texted Sha'Neka and told her that I found a new church home. I was beyond excited, and things just felt right. I knew it was where I was supposed to be. I had taken a big leap of faith and had been obedient even when it didn't make sense.

Although I had now found a new church home, I still felt obligated to have a discussion with my former Pastor about leaving the church. I was still serving in the youth choir and was the church clerk, so I felt that meeting with the Pastor formally to let him know my decision was the right thing to do. I scheduled a meeting with him on a Tuesday night. I had been sick to my stomach from nervousness and dreading the conversation. Although I knew that I had made the right decision and I was following what God had directed me to do, I felt like I was disappointing the Pastor. I felt like a young adult who was making the decision to leave and go to college far away from their family and was sitting down with their parents to break the news. This church, after all, had given me my spiritual foundation and I had grown to love and care for the Pastor as a father figure. I started off the conversation by telling him just that. I stated that I knew that God was leading me elsewhere and that leaving was an act of obedience to God.

The Paster sat there, very quiet, listening and showing no emotion towards me. I was crying because I felt like such a disappointment. I knew God was leading me, yet this man's opinion mattered so much to me that I felt the need to over-explain what I knew God was directing me to do. The Pastor's response was cold towards me, and I could tell that he was taking my departure personally. Remember, changes in other people very seldom have anything to do with us. Learn to depersonalize. Finally, after what felt like minutes, the pastor responded to me by asking, "Are you sure it's God that's directing you?"

His response floored me and offended me at the same time. Here he was, speaking to me as if I was completely incapable of hearing from God, as if God couldn't possibly be speaking to me. I was deeply saddened by the response and lack of support that I received, but more importantly, I was completely caught off-guard by how I felt guilty about letting down another human being when I was leaving to go where God was leading me. I was almost more afraid of disappointing him as my Pastor than I was of disappointing God.

When you attend a church for so long, you get to know the people, and naturally those people begin to feel like family. That was certainly the case for me. You admire and love your Pastor, as you should, and his opinion of you matters. While this is a very natural occurrence, we must be mindful and cautious of putting our Pastor, or any other person for that matter, above God. Respect and admire your Pastor, but don't worship your Pastor.

I started to attend my new church, called The Point Church. I loved the fact that the church focused on new believers in Christ, because after all, that was "the point." I have always been passionate about working with youth. I've always had the mindset to become the mentor that I wished I had when I was growing up. As a result, I got involved with the youth ministry at The Point. It's something I'm still involved with and still very passionate about. I also started

making new friends at church. I had the advantage of already knowing a few people from the choir I sang on, the Salt Lake City Mass
Choir. I found a new group of friends who welcomed me into their
circle with open arms and helped to make my transition easier. God
had provided another ram in the bush.

I called Sha'Neka one day while I was sitting in the church park-
ing lot waiting for Bible study to start. I told her how excited I was
about this new journey and how God was already blessing my life.
We talked about how we were going to continue to support each
other and help each other to walk in our God-given purposes. We
promised to be there for one another.

A few days later, Sha'Neka called me and told me that she felt
like I had been working too hard and I needed a break. She told me
that she had purchased tickets for us to see Xscape in concert. They
were doing a reunion tour and were scheduled to be in Oakland
California on January 5, 2018. We were in the process of planning
our weekend getaway down to booking the plane tickets and the
hotel rooms. Sha'Neka was scheduled to have a medical procedure
done right before our trip. She was confident that she had scheduled
enough time to have the procedure and recover before our trip.
Unfortunately, we never made that trip.

The last time I spoke to Sha'Neka was on Wednesday, January
24, 2018. She called me while I was at a lunch meeting with some
coworkers. I almost didn't answer, thinking that I would just call
her back later. I felt a strong urge to just answer the phone, so I
stepped outside of the restaurant and answered. She had her origi-
nal scheduled medical procedure already and was scheduled to have
a follow-up medical procedure that Friday. She called me to see if
I could bring her son Zay some lunch that day. I responded, "Of
course sis, you know I got you," to which she responded, "I know
you do, and I love you for that."

Sha'Neka was rushed to the hospital a few hours after that conversation and passed away on January 25, 2018. I was at the hospital when she passed away. I got to say my goodbyes to her and stood outside of her hospital room as we watched her heart rate on the heart monitor slowly decline until she was gone. To say I was devastated would be an understatement. Here I was *still* in the middle of my "wilderness period," feeling so alone, and God had taken away from me the one person who truly understood me and encouraged me. I didn't understand it. Sometimes I still struggle to understand it.

I know that God allowed Sha'Neka to come into my life for a purpose. She was there for me when I needed her the most. I know that I was part of Sha'Neka's purpose on the earth. While she is no longer physically here, she still manages to bless my life with the many encouraging text messages that she sent me, and the amazing family that she left behind, the people I now also call family. I have the honor and pleasure of being in Zay's life to this day. I get to watch him grow into the spitting image of his mother, both in her looks and in her personality. I cherish the time spent with the Daniels family. Remember that little girl who so desperately desired a family? Well, let's just say she's been blessed abundantly in that area of her life.

| eight |

The Healing Begins - Or Does It?

Healing is unfortunately a road that many of us don't take, or we attempt to skip past. We may jump from one romantic relationship to another in a poor attempt to ignore our pain. We may grow to develop a habit of "healing" through substance use and abuse, or sometimes we develop defense mechanisms to protect ourselves while negatively impacting our ability to heal.

Grief is a painful trauma; it's like a gruesome battle wound that never heals. I have spent the last ten years watching and nursing my grief, patiently waiting for it to heal. I can be driving in my car with the windows down, playing H.E.R. with the sun shining bright on me, completely in my happy place, and then boom! My mind brings up a memory or reminds me of the fact that I'm a childless mother, and that wound opens as if it's fresh all over again.

The challenging part about grief is that everyone has an opinion on how to grieve. There is no right way. Far too often, instead of helping others through their grief, we judge them for how they grieve. We look at a grieving person's actions and suddenly become experts on grief. "Why in the world is she doing that? Is she even sad? That is not the right way to handle things." True, it may not be the best way to handle things, but when you experience a loss that rocks you to your core, trust me, you're doing what makes sense to you in a world that makes no sense at all. Learn to be compassionate towards those who grieve. Nothing about loss makes sense, so why do we expect our reactions to loss to make sense?

For the longest time, I felt like something was wrong with me, like my healing 'thing-a-ma-gigger' is broken. I put so much pressure on myself to heal and no longer show the signs of a grieving mother. It was as if grief had an expiration date. I experienced my worst nightmare and somehow expected myself to just deal with it and move on. Learn to be compassionate towards yourself as you journey through grief.

One day, a few months ago, I was sitting on my couch watching a movie with my husband, completely relaxed, and suddenly the grief wound reopened. I went from being completely content, to having a thought about my daughter that took me right back to the day she died. It was in that moment that I realized that grieving may never stop, and the grief wound may never heal and that's okay. I'm not broken, I'm human, and I'm making the most of the cards that I've been dealt. When those moments hit, I'm committed to allow myself to feel, cry if I must, dust myself off and keep going. Guess what, IT'S OKAY!

It is possible to heal while still hurting. Healing is not the absence of the pain; it's learning how to manage that pain. Pain management is the process of improving your quality of life. The goal of pain management is not to heal the ailment causing the pain, but to make the pain manageable. That's the goal with healing as well. We can't change the grief or the trauma that caused our pain, but we can learn how to manage it. We can learn to live with it. When someone seeks out pain management, they typically start with an evaluation by the doctor. The doctor may provide interventions or methods to help with the pain. Then, often, the patient is asked to participate in the healing process through physical therapy which is meant to help with range of motion and strength.

Healing from trauma works in a similar manner. Your first step should be to seek out the guidance of the ultimate Doctor, and Healer, God. Your pain matters to Him, and He desires for us to be whole and healthy.

"For I know the plans I have for you, declares the Lord, plans to prosper you and not to harm you, plans to give you hope and a future." Jeremiah 29:11 NIV

He provides interventions, or methods to help with the pain through the Bible, pastors, and sometimes complete strangers; His methods are many. In addition to the resources that God provides, sometimes our healing requires a trained, licensed professional, in the form of a therapist.

You can have both God, and therapy. Seeking a therapist is not a reflection of your faith level with God. It reflects your desire to be healed, and a reflection of your willingness to participate in the healing process, just like physical therapy during pain management. While healing may not look how we expect it to look, it is possible.

During our healing process, there is a natural tendency to blame other people for what has happened in our lives. We must move away from this mindset. It's damaging and far too often it holds us back and prevents us from reaching our true destiny. With the things that happened to me as a child, I couldn't control the lies that were told about me, the consequences of those lies, or the sexual abuse and rape I experienced. However, as an adult, it became my responsibility to choose how I allowed those things to impact my future. This also became a necessary part of the healing process.

I don't mean to sound insensitive when I say this but hear me out. You cannot be a full-grown adult, blaming your current situation on what happened to you as a child. Yes, it happened, and it wasn't fair, but you are an adult now. You may not have chosen what happened to you, but you absolutely can control how it impacts your life moving forward. Get counseling, learn coping mechanisms, pray, and ask God to guide you. You're not alone in the journey.

The people who hurt you, and the circumstances that led to your trauma are unfortunately not going to help you heal. In fact, often, they are not even concerned with you. The healing falls on you. You've already been victimized, and you couldn't do anything about it. Let the trauma end there, and don't you dare continue to be victimized moving forward. Look in the mirror and tell yourself, "I deserve to be whole."

Overcoming trauma in one area doesn't make you exempt from trauma in other areas. As long as we are alive, the journey never gets easier. Just like with physical therapy, the more we experience the process of healing, the easier it becomes. The more we rely on God for our healing, the more we learn to trust Him. Before we know it, dealing with the effects of trauma becomes second nature.

"I have told you these things, so that in me you may have peace. In this world you will have trouble. But take heart! I have overcome the world."

John 16:33 NIV

Rest assured, He's with us through it all, and with Him, we will not fail.

| nine |

Intentional Living

What does it mean to live intentionally? If we look up the definition of intention, you may be surprised to find that one of the definitions of intention is "a healing process of a wound." (Oxford Languages) Insert "mind blown" emoji here. I've never heard that definition before. The other definition of intention is "a thing intended, an aim or a plan." The root word of intent comes from the Latin word "tendere" which means to "stretch or extend." So, one could say that in summary, to live intentionally means to go through the process of healing by stretching and/or extending yourself.

God is faithful; I have no doubt about it - but what happens when it feels like your prayers aren't being answered? Did He check out? Is He too busy answering the prayers of everyone else? The desire to have another child is strong and the older I get the more I start to doubt that it will happen. When Desirae died, God made me a promise, and that promise was that I would have another child. He didn't tell me when, or how long I would have to wait, but He made me a promise. It is not our place to know when and how something will happen; it is our job to trust God. Sometimes the test is waiting. Has God promised you something that hasn't yet come to pass? Are you waiting for that child to be born, for a marriage, or for a shift in your current circumstances? What are you doing while you wait? In account after account in the Bible we see people waiting for a promise from God to be fulfilled and most of the time that promise is fulfilled while they are serving the Lord. Paul instructed Timothy to "be prepared in season and out of season" 2nd Timothy 4:2 (NIV) - in other words, be prepared to serve regardless of the season. As you serve the Lord, waiting for your promises to be fulfilled becomes a lot easier.

I've learned the importance of being intentional in serving. If we are not careful, we can serve in ways that are detrimental to our progress. Serving does not mean saying yes to everything that comes your way. After Desirae died, I experienced a strong desire to serve. I both needed and wanted to draw close to God. Before I knew it, I was teaching Sunday School, serving as a deaconess, and operating as church clerk. Was I serving? Absolutely! Was I serving productively and being fruitful? That's a hard NO!

It's one thing to be intentional in your serving, it's another thing to be intentional in your living. Due to my desire to be married, I had become a serial dater. I met men through dating websites, at the grocery store, and through social networks. I loved the excitement and thrill of dating. By dating, I'm not referring to having sex, hooking up, or the classic "Netflix and Chill' but true dating. Boy meets girl, swipes right or asks her out, girl agrees, boy and girl go out for dinner and/or drinks, boy and girl continue dating, boy and girl enter the relationship; boy and girl break up after one to two years of dating, and then REPEAT. This was my cycle for years. Getting into a relationship was never the issue, staying in the relationship and being intentional about where the relationship was going is where I had trouble.

While I desired to be married, I was horrible at being intentional about dating. Let's not get things twisted, I never dated ugly men,

I just seldom took the opportunity to ask the intentional questions when getting to know someone. We needed to ask deeper questions than, "What's your favorite color?" or "Do you like breakfast foods?" Dating was easy for me, and I was perfectly okay with only knowing people on the surface. It was a lot less complicated that way. I should have been asking questions like, "What is your relationship with God?" (The standard "Do you go to church?" isn't enough), "What are your goals?" and the question of all questions, "WHERE IS THIS RELATIONSHIP GOING?"

Due to not being intentional in my relationships, I had a wide range of dating experiences, to say the least. One man had a WHOLE fiancé while he was dating me. There was a wedding proposal that involved the man sending my engagement ring via FEDEX because we had gotten into an argument, and he had left the state to "cool off." A military man wanted me to move to Connecticut with him just to be a girlfriend who he "might want to marry" when he retired from the military in ten to fifteen years… and unfortunately, I had a couple of situationships/entanglements too.

I finally had enough of dating and wasting the precious time that God had gifted to me. I started going to the gym, working on myself, and just focusing on me. I was truly single for the first time in years. I was no longer focused on marriage and was living my best Kingdom life. It was of course during this time of "me" that my current husband entered my life.

In December 2018, a friend of mine was preparing to move out of Utah. She hosted a going-away party, and the crowd was the usual people that we hung out with - except that Terron was there. I knew him from church, but I didn't know much about him. We'd had a few very small conversations, and I found him to be flirty at times, but he showed no real interest that I could detect. He was handsome, or whatever, but I wasn't really looking for anyone, so to me, on that night, he was just the guy from church. I thought that he was in a relationship. The party ended, and most of the guests had left except for my immediate group of friends (my "circle family"), and Terron. I thought nothing of it. Terron never held a direct conversation with me the entire night; he was quiet, and we were all just conversing as usual. I had no idea that Terron was observing me.

A few days later, I got a text from my friend Mercedes; her husband and Terron were working together. The text said, "Hey, what do you think about Terron?" I responded, "He's pretty cool, but he flirts a lot for a married man." Six months prior, Terron had been attending church with a lady, and I had somehow assumed that he was married. In hindsight, I was still not catching on to the fact that Terron was interested, but I clearly felt some type of way about this "married" man flirting with me. Mercedes' response to me was, "He's not married," to which I replied, "Yes, I'm pretty sure he is." Mercedes reassured me that he wasn't to which I finally replied, "Oh, well he's cool I guess." I don't know what kind of mood I was in on that day, but Terron clearly didn't stand a chance. I guess Mercedes realized that because she stopped texting me. A few days later, I received a text from her that said, "Don't be mad, I gave Terron your number, love you bye!"

Terron texted me a few hours later, and we made plans to go on a date that weekend. Do you guys know that this man was four hours late for our first date??? He kept texting me and pushing back the time that he was going to come get me. I was so mad, because I was looking really cute, but something kept telling me to just go, so I did. I later found out that he wasn't sure about going on a date with me because he thought I was "high maintenance." He kept talking himself out of going on the date before finally deciding to pick me up. The joke was on him because about an hour into our date he told me, "You're one of the most chill people I've ever met." Duh, and to think we almost never happened.

Terron kept the details of our first date a secret. He simply picked me up and asked me to just go along for the ride. It ended up being the best first date that I had ever experienced.

We started hanging out on a regular basis after that. Most of our dates involved long drives and conversations. Terron was different from most men. He never put pressure on me to have sex. He was genuinely more interested in having a conversation and getting to know me than he was interested in having sex.

Terron was intentional with me. He made it very clear early on that he wasn't dating for fun. He wanted a wife, and he saw the qualities that he needed in a wife in me. I never had to question where I stood with him or where the relationship was going. I never even had to initiate the conversation about where we were going.

We certainly faced our challenges during those initial months of dating; we saw each other in every possible light. After eleven months of dating and dropping hints to friends and families that one day we would just pop up married, we did just that. In a private ceremony in Las Vegas, Nevada I became Mrs. Howell. We immediately told friends, family, and our Pastor that we wed, but by the time the rest of the world knew, we had already enjoyed over a month of happy, private, wedded bliss. Intentionally.

Nothing requires more intentionality than marriage. You must intentionally make the choice to show up and be present in your marriage. Just like any other aspect in life, marriage does not consist of perfect people. Marriage in its simplest definition is two imperfectly flawed people who are committed to work with each other in navigating life. Marriage is service to one another. If you aim to serve your partner always, and they do the same, you will have a successful marriage. I'm convinced that no matter how difficult things get, if you are willing to work on things, and your spouse is willing to work on things, you can accomplish anything.

Along with marrying Terron, I got another great gift, Terron's son Elijah. He was two years old when I came into his life. He's the smartest, most amazing child, and one of the biggest blessings of my life. I call him my bonus-son and he refers to me lovingly as his "Mom-Tawn." He has always pronounced my name "Tawn" and I've never bothered to correct him. In fact, I pray that no matter how old he gets, he continues to refer to me as "Tawn."

I began to be intentional in my work too. Our work serves a purpose and God can and will use you on your job for His glory. I never intended on working in human resources. I wanted to be a social worker due to the great example that Mrs. Bernice provided me. I even graduated from college with a degree in Human Service Management with an emphasis on Children and Family. I was determined to be the next Mrs. Bernice, but God had already predestined a career path that would be all my own.

"May the favor of the Lord our God rest on us; establish the work of our hands for us - yes, establish the work of our hands." Psalms 90:17 (NIV)

Shortly after Desirae passed away, I was hired as a Concierge/Receptionist at a senior living home. I had spent the previous seven years of my life as a customer service representative in a call center and even though I frequently switched companies, hoping to find something better, the work was miserable and I knew it wouldn't be a long-term solution for me. The work at the senior living home was a breath of fresh air. It involved me sitting at the front desk greeting visitors, and my favorite part, listening to the seniors tell me stories about their lives. I remember getting the job and telling my adoptive mom that, "Something felt different about this role; it just felt like something bigger was coming from it." I was right, and still to this day I seek out that same feeling before I take on a new position or job.

When I started, I was trained by a girl who was set to go out on maternity leave any day. She was the assistant to our boss, the Business Office Director. She trained me on how to cover some of her assistant tasks while she was away, which included a lot of HR administrative tasks. Although my role was very administrative, I enjoyed learning about the human resources function. The young lady who trained me never returned from maternity leave, and I was promoted to her position. Shortly after that, my boss left the company, and I was promoted into her position which combined business office and human resources duties.

The more I learned about human resources, the more I enjoyed it. I've never been afraid to have difficult conversations and I found that I had the ability to have those difficult conversations with employees and leave them feeling good about the conversation. The deep voice that kids used to make fun of me for was calming to others and made them feel at ease. My ability to see God's hand in everything helped others to also recognize His presence and see His hand in everything, even if they didn't realize that they were experiencing God. These interactions planted a seed of who God is and what His presence felt like in their lives.

I continued to grow in my career and sought out job opportunities that allowed me to accelerate. I learned that human resources was more than just administrative office work. It was about people interaction, helping others to navigate difficult situations, and helping those in senior leadership to recognize the need to take care of the people in their organization. I realized that I could use this career to truly help others, so I became intentional about excelling in my craft. I studied hard and became a certified human resource professional. I learned that being intentional about my career required me to invest in myself.

Through those investments I was blessed to work my way up in various companies, working alongside the executives of the company while ensuring that the people in the company, those who made the company, were cared for, and protected. I strived to share my perspective of human resources that I experienced in my early working career. I made it my goal to help others as much as possible in every interaction that I had with them, and to break all negative stereotypes of human resources professionals. Nothing compared to the feeling I had when I was able to help an employee navigate through a sticky personal or work situation, or when I was able to show compassion to them as employees, and to help them to grow as leaders. I had found my happy place at work.

"Do everything in love" 1 Corinthians 16:14 (NIV)

I took a chance on myself and relied on God to provide for me in every work environment. God provided for me, and I believe it happened because in my heart I wanted to help others. I worked my way up from my first human resources job in a senior living center, to a human resources manager, to a director of human resources, and in March 2022, I became a vice president of human resources.

"Whatever you do, work at it with all your heart, as working for the Lord, not for human masters, since you know that you will receive an inheritance from the Lord as a reward. It is the Lord Christ you are serving." Colossians 3:23-24(NIV)

Pray over your career goals and decisions, trust God to provide for you, invest in your career and in your future, then determine what makes you happy and pursue it. Be intentional about your career decisions.

"And God is able to bless you abundantly, so that in all things at all times, having all that you need, you will abound in every good work." 2 Corinthians 9:8 (NIV)

When you learn to be intentional in your life, things start to happen - not only to you, but for you. Being intentional requires your involvement; you must take charge of life rather than just waiting for life to happen to you. Invest in yourself through career development and education, seeking therapy to help you address your traumas and to heal, and investing in the healthy relationships that you have in your life. Be intentional about living, be intentional about healing, and be intentional about finding the necessity in your trauma.

| ten |

My Prayer for You

I didn't write this book because I know everything, and I figured out everything. I wrote this book as an act of obedience to God. After writing this book, there's not a guarantee that I will remember to follow the guidance that God poured out through me on these pages the next time I face trauma. There's a good chance that even as the author of this book, I may need to be reminded of the things written here at some point in my life.

The same applies to you as the reader of the book. There is no quick cure or fix for the trauma that we experience in life, and there's no way to escape trauma. I'm not a therapist, and I will never portray myself to be one. The only thing that I know without a doubt about trauma is that God can use it for our good, and He can trade beauty for ashes. I know that despite our life circumstances, God wants more and better for us. I know that He can show you how the trauma in your life was necessary, and He uses that trauma to bring us closer to our destinies.

Chances are you were drawn to this book because you relate to some of my trauma, or someone may have recommended this book to you. My hope in writing this book is that you might evaluate the situations that have happened in your life, and that you may seek the wisdom of God in understanding the purpose behind every situation, good or bad. I pray that you would allow God to heal the painful areas of your life and give you the strength to face the dark parts of your life. So much of our life happens to us without our consent; most are things that we could not control. We couldn't control what happened to us, but we can control how we move forward. As I finish this book, I feel led to pour out a prayer that God has placed on my heart. I pray that you will read this prayer, meditate on it, and allow it to be as real for you as it is for me.

Abba, Father, my Healer, my Provider, and my Protector, I come to you heavy in heart because of the experiences that life has presented to me. I feel the weight of the world on my shoulders. I'm hurting and seeking refuge in You. Give me the strength and courage to address the sore spots in my heart: the spots that I keep secret and covered, and the things I bury so that I don't have to address them. I take those things God, and I lay them at Your feet so that You can fix those broken pieces. I lay them at your feet along with every negative thought, emotion, and feeling that I've carried with them. Every unspoken apology that I will never receive from those who hurt me, every feeling of guilt and blame over the things that I may have caused, and every ill will and bad intention that I harbor against those who hurt me - I lay it all at your feet. I SURREN-DER it all to you. I leave those things at Your feet, and I pick up Your love - the love that you have for me, and the things that you have spoken over me in Your Word. This includes the things that You say that I am, but I have never chosen to believe. Teach me to love me in the way that You love me. Teach me to see me how You see me. Teach me to desire the things that You want for my life and help me to be intentional in pursuing those things. Teach me how to love others in the same way that

You love them. Give me the desire to pray for those who have hurt me, even if the prayer is just, "Lord, help them." Teach me to look beyond their actions and flaws and see who You created them to be. Fill my heart with the knowledge of who You are and what You can do. Help me to rely on You for all things because You can, and You will provide for me. Heal the broken pieces of me, so that the traumas that have engulfed me can no longer have power or control over me. I surrender my trauma to You. Help me to see how my traumas were necessary. Help me to be intentional about living my life, blessed by You. Align me with Your will and Your purpose for my life. Order my steps, God, and may my moves and plans for my life be in sync with You.

In the name of Jesus, I pray,

Amen.

| eleven |

Acknowledgements

First and foremost, thank you, God! You are faithful, and I praise you for all that you are. I am nothing without you, and I have nothing without you. Thank you, Jesus, for paying the ultimate price so that I can have life to the fullest. I give you all the glory, honor, and praise!

To my husband Terron, thank you for your continued love and support. You are truly my number one supporter. You constantly remind me to take a deep breath, slow down, and just live in the moment. For that, I'm thankful. I love you tons.

To my bonus son Elijah, it is such a blessing to be part of your life. Watching you grow and become the awesome, smart, sweet, and kind young man that you are has been one of the greatest joys of my life. I love you beyond words, and I'm so proud of the person you are becoming.

To the Hadley and Larsen families, thank you for welcoming me into your families and hearts with open arms. Utah may not be my favorite place, but being here has brought me so many opportunities, and I wouldn't be here without you.

To Sha'Neka, I love and miss you every day. Thank you for guiding me through one of the hardest moments of my life. Your presence in my life was no coincidence, it was a touch from God. Thank you for the support system you left me here on earth. They are truly my family, and I will always hold them down for you. Until we meet again sis, I LOVE you!

To my faith community, and friends THANK YOU. This book was incredibly hard to write, the many texts, calls, and check-ins to see how the book was going were much appreciated. I couldn't have made it without you all.

www.ingramcontent.com/pod-product-compliance
Lightning Source LLC
Chambersburg PA
CBHW040922110726

48006CB00001B/32